Power, Morals, and the Founding Fathers:

Essays in the Interpretation of the American Enlightenment

Power, Morals, and the Founding Fathers

Essays in the Interpretation of
the American Enlightenment

By Adrienne Koch

Cornell Paperbacks

Cornell University Press

ITHACA AND LONDON

First printing for Great Seal Books 1961

Second printing 1963

Third printing, Cornell Paperbacks, 1966

Fourth printing, clothbound, 1967

Fifth printing, Cornell Paperbacks, 1967

Sixth printing 1969

STANDARD BOOK NUMBER: 8014-9019-7
LIBRARY OF CONGRESS CATALOG CARD NUMBER: 61-12995

PRINTED IN THE UNITED STATES OF AMERICA
BY VAIL-BALLOU PRESS, INC.

In loving memory of my father,

JOHN DESIDER KOCH

Preface

THIS volume assembles a group of essays that have appeared in various journals over a period of ten years. They are unified in their treatment of two main themes. One focuses on an interpretation of the American Enlightenment and those aspects in the thought and character of the founding fathers which conjoin the supposedly contradictory terms "power" and "morals." The other theme centers on what I believe is still vital and viable about the political and moral tradition they hoped to establish.

These essays serve to emphasize certain features of the American Enlightenment that are often obscured or given a false perspective. Franklin, as the progenitor and, in Jefferson's phrase, "the father of American philosophy," helps to delineate the American Enlightenment's underlying attitude of pragmatic wisdom. Jefferson's contribution is seen against the political, moral, and personal implications of his "right to the pursuit of happiness." The essay on Hamilton centers on the pursuit of power, both in its economic implications for political growth and in its personal aspects in his own career. John Adams, both as "John Yankee" and as the "Atlas of Independence," is viewed as preoccupied with the taming of power. And finally, Madison's efforts are neatly symbolized by his image of America as the workshop of liberty. In all these figures the conjunction of power with morals results in a vision of America and an attitude of experimental humanism which may still serve in a time of crisis. The present significance of their thought and work is pointed out in the course of the five essays on the founding fathers but is given more explicit treatment in the last two essays.

The inclusion of these essays in one volume called for some adaptation and redivision in order to avoid overlapping and repetition. In the spring of 1952 the basic materials were delivered as a series of lectures under the auspices of the Committee on International Relations at the University of Notre Dame. The lectures were later printed in successive issues of the *Review of Politics,* in October, 1953, and January and April, 1954. They form the core of the present matter in Chapters III, IV, V, and VI and appear as portions of Chapters I and VII.

The provenance of the other materials in the essays is as follows: The introductory Chapter I contains portions of the lead article in the February 21, 1960, issue of the *New York Times Book Review* entitled "Men Who Made Our Nation What It Is." In addition, Chapters I, II, and III incorporate sections of an address given at the Christmas, 1959, meeting of the American Historical Association under the title "The American Enlightenment and Pragmatic Wisdom." Chapter IV includes matter from my article, "Hamilton and Power," printed in the *Yale Review,* Summer, 1958. Chapter V reprints matter from my introduction to *The Selected Writings of John and John Quincy Adams,* edited with William Peden and published in 1946 by Alfred A. Knopf, Inc. Chapter VII is based upon an article from the Winter, 1952, issue of the *Yale Review* and includes sections of my article, "The Status of Values and Democratic Political Theory," in *Ethics,* April, 1958. Chapter VIII was delivered as an address at the 1952 meeting of the Southern Historical Association and was printed in the *Virginia Quarterly Review,* Spring, 1953.

I am grateful to the editors of the foregoing periodicals and to Alfred A. Knopf, Inc., for their kind permission to reprint these materials. In addition, I should like to voice my appreciation of the kindness of the late Waldemar Gurian in graciously inviting me to give the original set of lectures which form the core of these essays; of Clinton Rossiter for suggesting that the essays be reprinted; and of my husband, Lawrence R. Kegan, for giving me the benefit of his constant and devoted criticism in every phase in the preparation of these essays.

ADRIENNE KOCH

Berkeley, California
January 1961

Contents

I   Introduction 1

II   Franklin and Pragmatic Wisdom 14

III   Jefferson and the Pursuit of Happiness 23

IV   Hamilton and the Pursuit of Power 50

V   Adams and the Taming of Power 81

VI   Madison and the Workshop of Liberty 103

VII   The Idea of America 122

VIII   Toward an American Philosophy 138

Index 153

Power, Morals, and the Founding Fathers:

Essays in the Interpretation of the American Enlightenment

CHAPTER I

Introduction

A FEW words may be in order at the outset to explain why I have chosen the title *Power, Morals, and the Founding Fathers*. I believe that we can learn much from an inquiry into the basic thought and character of the statesmen of the Republic that may help us in meeting the crisis of a divided world today. And such an inquiry can be most effectively pursued by a consideration of their views on power and morals.

Of the first statesmen of the Republic, five—Franklin, John Adams, Jefferson, Madison, and, to a lesser extent, Hamilton—trained their sights higher than did any others. Addressing themselves to more than practical considerations, they seemed to be genuinely inspired by the historical uniqueness of the experience open to them—that of launching a new experiment in self-government. They were philosopher-statesmen: they heeded the double drive of philosophy and leadership, thought and action, vision and its fortifying concrete detail. In their different ways they dedicated themselves to forming and strengthening the union because they believed it was good. In final outcome they proved equal to the challenge of planning republican government because they tried to understand, not only the buried sources of power, but the moral objectives of good government. Their principles, even when account is taken of the differences among them, collectively help to define the range of our national ideology—our objectives, our character as a people, our economic and social patterns, our American way of life.

The thought and character of these statesmen sharply contrast with that of the founding fathers of the Soviet Union. Lenin, Trotsky, and Stalin considered themselves to be philosopher-statesmen, but their philosophy was dialectically intolerant of any differences of thought; the differences that did arise were ultimately seen as total and therefore had to eventuate in the victory of one man, who was then deified. Stalin attained his ascendancy by liquidating practically every one of the founding fathers associated with him after the death of Lenin and by establishing a totalitarian religion, with its sacred texts, official interpretations, and church hierarchy. The Russian founding fathers, too, viewed their work as an experiment, but it was one that subordinated moral values to power and reduced men to the mass, to agents to be used by the secular god for ends determined by him to be necessary and, therefore, good. And, finally, they too were dedicated to unity, but it was a monolithic unity associated with the power to enforce total fear and terror.

It is evident that the Communist way of life is opposed to the democratic way of life, and that a closed society implies a view of power and morals that is incompatible with that of an open society. The two greatest powers in the world today, the United States and the Soviet Union, embody these opposing philosophies, and the outcome of their efforts to establish and secure their views of society is critical for the future of man's career on earth. As a result of this crisis we are forced to reflect on the issues of power and morals—on whether power can be successful only if it is exercised without concern for moral considerations. How we, who inherit the American tradition, pursue these reflections will partly influence man's fate. I propose to explore the hypotheses that the American experiment in democracy, as envisaged by the founding fathers, does involve the exercise of power to protect and promote the common good and that the strongest, because most durable, government derives its power from the consent of free men.

1

There is another reason for such reflections today. If there is truth in the view that ideas and theories originate in *felt difficulties,* then I would suggest that there is work to be done to understand the nature of the American Enlightenment. For it is more than ordinarily disconcerting to consult the accounts of this important period of intellectual adventure and to find a portrait whose focus distorts the reality. The range of interpretations that offer themselves as descriptions of this unparalleled period of American thought appear to make one fundamental charge: that this thought is dogmatic.

Some historians maintain that American Enlightenment thought is dogmatic in so emphasizing reason that it becomes the "cult" of reason. Thus, Carl Becker treats Enlightenment thought as dogmatic in its resort to reason and to the presence of a determinative element that might be called secular religion. This theme provides the governing paradox in his celebrated study, *The Heavenly City of the Eighteenth-Century Philosophers.*

Other historians trace the dogma to its source in something like the "given" of experience. This view is illustrated by more recent interpretations of the American Enlightenment which emerge from studies whose focus is not necessarily on that period per se, such as Louis Hartz's book on *The Liberal Tradition in America* and Daniel Boorstin's *The Americans: The Colonial Experience.* Here the emphasis is on the uniqueness of American conditions—the absence of a feudal past, the availability of extensive land, the lack of interest in and the incapacity for systematic theory or philosophy. Experience, the given, with its more or less random exploitation, is the secret of American civilization.

A corollary to these views of the American Enlightenment as one or another sort of dogma, whether of absolute reason or absolute experience, is the charge that it is essentially un-historical—failing either to recognize the value of tradition or to suggest the qualitative sense of history. For reason is understood by those who make the charge to mean *abstract, a priori* reason, whereas experience is similarly confined to the immediate, particularistic, and unique. And on such premises, where reason is *empty* reason and experience is *blind* experience, historical connections and transitions, including tradition, cannot matter in the least!

These essays do not engage in a negative critique of the interpretations I have roughly typified but provide an alternative interpretation of a more reliable sort. In my interpretation the founding fathers must serve as touchstones for the character of the American Enlightenment. They are universally conceded to be the fullest embodiments of the spirit of the Enlightenment in America, and their intellectual and personal eminence among their contemporaries is confirmed by the tributes American and world society have continued to pay to them. Any proposed interpretation of the American Enlightenment would shipwreck if it failed to account for their characteristic pattern of thought and principles of action.

My main theme is that no headway can be made in understanding the American Enlightenment until we conjoin "theory" and "experience." It is true that Plato and Aristotle separate knowledge as *theoria* from experience as *praxis,* and this philosophical split seems to underlie the range of previous interpretations that have been offered. But this split is false when seen in the philosophical perspective associated with the rise of modern science. The Platonic-Aristotelian disjunction is challenged by the Baconian experimental theory. And it is this Baconian challenge, when applied not only to the order of physical nature but also to the human order of morals and politics, that feeds into the stream which is the specific tradition to which the American Enlightenment—and the founding fathers—belong. Significant influences in that stream are the Socratic injunction for self-knowledge, the benevolent model of the humane Jesus, and the humanist view of wisdom as a full active life of man.

These essays point out certain essential features of the American Enlightenment that center about the supposedly contradictory pairs of terms, "pragmatic" and "wisdom," "power" and "morals." By conjoining these pairs of terms I want to show that the normal use of them as somehow antithetical is unwarranted, and that the American Enlightenment, at least, cannot be understood on the basis of the kind of protocol which demands that they be kept apart. For the American Enlightenment was characterized in its thought by its profound attachment to experimental empiricism and its equally profound attachment to the humanistic ideal of the whole man, whose knowledge is not fragmented, nor fragmentary, but moral or ethical in its concern for man and his world. Since labels, though obnoxious, are helpful shorthand, we may call the central vision of the founding fathers and the temper of the Enlightenment in America "experimental humanism."

This vision is given concrete expression in the words of George Washington. He wrote not simply as the soldier-statesman but as the political leader who was to become the moderator of an active and sometimes divided philosophical company. At the end of the War of Independence, he was concerned with its political outcome, and in June, 1783, addressed a circular letter to the governors of the thirteen states with the hopeful prophecy that the future of the Republic would be assured if the union of the states could be preserved.

The foundation of our Empire was not laid in the gloomy age of ignorance and superstition, but at an Epoch when the rights of mankind were better understood and more clearly defined, than at any former period; the researches of the human mind after social happiness, have been carried to a great extent, the treasures of knowledge, acquired by the labours of Philosophers, Sages and Legislators, through a long succession of years, are laid open for our use, and their collected wisdom may be happily applied in the establishment of our forms of Government. . . . At this auspicious period, the United States came into existence as a Nation, and if their Citizens should not be completely free and happy, the fault will be intirely their own.

2

After the new republic of the United States was launched under the American Constitution, an event intruded itself into the anxious honeymoon of Washington's first administration about which the Constitution was silent but which goes to the heart of these reflections. I am referring, of course, to the rise of political parties—the division of the four statesmen (Hamilton and John Adams, Jefferson and Madison) and their followers into two political camps that did not become explicit and avowed on organizational lines until 1791. What is the significance of the Constitution's silence on political parties and the party division among those devoted to the republican experiment? Were the framers of the Constitution unaware that parties would exist, or were they trying to construct a monolithic party state which somehow slipped out from under their control? And were the two original parties simply concerned with the age-old skirmish of the ins and the outs, or did they reflect ponderable differences on the central issues of power and morals?

There is one important fact about the American political situation of the decade prior to the Constitutional Convention that provides, I think, the conclusive answer to the first question I raised a moment ago. Widespread dissatisfaction with the ineffectual Articles of Confederation had inspired young statesmen like Hamilton and Madison to agitate for a strong national union. They employed every means at their disposal—detailed argument in person and in letters to influential people, active membership in the Continental Congress, deliberate promotion of the Annapolis Convention, and, when that failed, the Federal Convention in Philadelphia—to secure more power for the national government. There was no lack of awareness of political differences over all matters of national concern. It was, indeed, this awareness that led the delegates who appeared at the Federal Convention to hold their sessions in secret, behind locked doors and closed windows despite the intense and unusual heat of the summer of 1787. Otherwise, they felt, the political cleavages might wreck the work of hammering out a document—work involving debate and committee activity—before the document could appear in finished form for ratification by the jealous sovereign states, whose citizens, for the first time, were to be united as "We, the people . . ."

We see, then, that the debate on the Constitution had behind it the reality of political opposition. This opposition was not sufficiently organized to be called a party in the technical sense, but it was organized enough to demarcate federalist and antifederalist. The main issue of the *Federalist Papers,* as seen by its two major authors, Hamilton and Madison, was to persuade the states to ratify the Constitution, so as to give more power to the nation in order to secure the interests of the people. They explicitly recognized the existence of factions and the resulting diverse political interests that arise naturally in every free government. Thus, when the Republic became an actuality, there was already a broad range of political thought and principle which crystallized, in a very short time, into the two political parties—Republican and Federalist. Both parties professed their attachment to the principles of the Republic. Hamilton and John Adams, as leaders of the Federalist Party, were devoted to the cause of liberty, as they saw it, but their ground and their vision were different from those of Jefferson and Madison, the leaders of the Republican Party.

As philosopher-statesmen, these four men each brought a different perspective to the American nation in its first years. An appreciation of their differences is important in appraising the richness of the ideology that has left its mark on the character and course of our nation. I should like to suggest, then, that we imagine a continuum, broadly called republicanism, without which the political contests of that day would come to us as dehydrated and meaningless external details out of a dead past. Actually, those contests were over fundamental moral and political principles, and real, live alternatives in the future of democracy. Indeed, the decade of the 1790's was a momentous one. The new government had just been established and was more precarious than it would ever be again. It obviously did not have the solidity of long precedent and tradition, and it could have taken one or another fatal turn. Those who were leading the American people declared themselves to be in a trackless wilderness without a single footstep to guide them. Their perplexities about infusing the Constitution with life under an operating government cannot help but move us even today.

The American experiment could have proved itself unsteady, unworkable, unworthy of further trial. Or it could have worn quite a different character. But it was the contest and conjunction of the four statesmen under the popular command of Washington that succeeded in establishing a strong national government dedicated, and since then continually rededicated, to the equal rights of man. And an important part of their success was due to the establishment of the political truths that a one-party state is a dictatorship; that there is no monopoly on political right, insight, ways, and means; that, accordingly, there should be no monopoly on political power; and that those who challenge the prevailing power, so long as they conform to the fundamental rules of an open society, are not conspirators to be silenced, crushed, or annihilated. The majority will is something more than dumb show; it is a real act of political choice. In short, just

as personal freedom necessitates the presence of real alternatives which can be scrutinized prior to intelligent action, so
political freedom requires the diversity of political parties to
make government by consent an operational reality. These
truths were won out of the political battles in which the first
statesmen of the Republic engaged. It is my purpose to deal
with these issues as reflected in the character and thought of
the founding fathers.

3

We of the 1960's should come to know more fully than we
could before the lives of those men whose character and ideas
were the building blocks of the American political tradition.
For today there is under way an unprecedented program for
the comprehensive publication of the papers of great American
statesmen. The year 1959 saw not only the issue of Volume XV
in the projected fifty-odd-volume edition of *The Papers of
Thomas Jefferson,* but also the appearance of the first volume
of the papers of Franklin. The year 1961 will witness the publication of four volumes of John Adams' diary and memoirs—
the opening phase of a massive enterprise bringing out the
papers of all important members of the Adams family—and
the first volume of the papers of James Madison. These are
simply the first fruits of a rich harvest. Editorial projects already in progress and others still to be established will include
the papers of Alexander Hamilton and documentary histories
of the ratification of the Constitution and of the First Congress
under the Constitution.

This current program for the publication of historical documents was sparked a decade ago, on May 17, 1950, when the
first volume of the new edition of *The Papers of Thomas
Jefferson* was presented to President Truman. Pointing out
that we face the greatest challenge in our history, Mr. Truman
charged the National Historical Publications Commission
with the task of preparing a plan "to collect and publish the

writings of the men and women who have made major contributions to the development of our democracy." He stipulated that the main effort should be undertaken by private groups and hoped that financial support would be forthcoming for publications that could maintain "the same high editorial standards that are evident in this first volume of *The Papers of Thomas Jefferson.*"

The primary result of this program will be to present, more completely and reliably than any earlier age would have dreamed to be possible, a picture of the American Enlightenment and of the efforts that launched the American experiment in democracy. The first part of the national program will focus on the "Big Five"—Jefferson, Franklin, Adams, Madison, and Hamilton—on the incontestable ground that the merit and range of their thought on fundamental questions require a broad presentation of their papers. Many may have felt that the writings of these founders, published in the fullness of correspondence to them as well as letters and essays by them, would result in a kind of informal encyclopedia of the American Enlightenment—one which would show the American philosopher-statesmen, in their experimental use of theory, as something different from philosophers of the French, German, or British Enlightenment.

To put out "comprehensive" editions of these papers, each project editor had to make a preparatory search for all the extant manuscripts. Such a search must be conducted heroically, sometimes cunningly; papers have to be pried loose from public and private holders and traced to an infinite variety of hiding places. One editor has called this early phase "the prowl." The prowl is worth its rigors. For example, the last (and largest) previous edition of Thomas Jefferson's writings published roughly 15 per cent of the total documents that will be found in the new edition of the Jefferson papers. The more than 50,000 documents that will go into this edition were drawn from about 425 different sources, including libraries, archives, governmental agencies, historical societies, schools, clubs, banks, commercial firms, dealers, at least one Indian reservation, foreign libraries and collections, and nearly 250 private owners of Jefferson documents. Imagine any would-be Jefferson scholar, however determined, however brilliant, trying to locate these sources without the organizational apparatus, the photo-duplication techniques, and the systematic files of a long-range editorial enterprise!

With *The Papers of Thomas Jefferson* functioning as the model for the new comprehensive editions, the editors of the Franklin, Adams, Madison, and Hamilton papers have followed suit with comparable results. The editor of the Madison papers has estimated that not more than one-quarter of the extant writings of James Madison has ever been published before. Lyman Butterfield, the editor of the Adams family papers, estimates that if anything like the Jefferson model of comprehensiveness were used, his edition would run to more than one hundred volumes.

The Franklin papers should run to about forty volumes, the outcome of a search that amassed about 20,000 documents, of which some 6,000 were of Franklin's authorship. The largest previous edition contained about 2,000 documents, nearly all of them by Franklin himself. Hamilton, on the other hand, obliged his editors by dying young on the field of "honor," so the collection of his papers should result in a relatively compact set.

The contemporary editor of such great collections of papers needs more than patience, perseverance, and the art of cajolery in extracting manuscripts from their hidden lairs; more than the luck that throws new materials into centralized editorial files; and more even than the organizational skill that masters the complex problems of creating a system of effective communication out of a hoard of miscellaneous papers, including fragmentary and mutilated records. The contemporary editor must bring to his task the highest order of historical knowledge, judgment, and that creative insight without which pioneers in scientific thought, as in art, are helpless.

In time, as the volumes multiply and the projects come to completion in the national historical publications program, one can anticipate the grumble of the unimaginative, "tough-minded" academician. Is it likely, these men will argue, that in a busy world anyone will have the time to read fifty volumes of Jefferson, or forty of Franklin—not to mention the shelf space to house the books?

Of course one might reply that no one will (or should) read through these mountainous tomes on a holiday or in a devouring frenzy, as some (I am told) consume Mickey Spillane. This is not to say that for the scholar or motivated student the contents of these volumes are lacking in fascination; on the contrary, they are, for this fortunate group, of infinite charm and immeasurable worth. The purpose of the publishing program is naturally not to provide a competitor for the book clubs' current selections. Rather, the great and proper purpose is to increase the "avenues of knowledge" of ourselves, our traditions, and the meaning of the American experiment.

John Adams grasped the essence of this kind of situation when he wrote, "Know thyself is as useful a precept to nations as to men." If these publications are to have this value, we, the people, must also take to heart Goethe's wise admonition that "whatever you cannot understand, you cannot possess." The will to understand and use the splendid hoards that will be opened to us is the ultimate test of the vitality of our belief in American traditions. It has been said that America, in the era when democratic thought was being formulated, conducted one of the most informed public debates on the nature of free institutions ever to grace the annals of any nation.

These materials will be accessible for the first time, for all to study. But we will also be able to encounter, behind the institutions, the human beings who shaped them; to savor the accidents of speech, the variations of mood, the climate of ideas; to comprehend what worried these statesmen, what held their aspirations, how they fought and developed, and how they summed up the meaning of life. The failures, as well as the successes, of leaders who desired something greater than personal power are themselves full of human and public meaning.

To share in the knowledge, the faith, and the life of men like Jefferson, Madison, and John Adams is to learn what it means to be a citizen in a free republic—the system of liberty and power which these early philosopher-statesmen made work.

CHAPTER II

Franklin and Pragmatic Wisdom

A USEFUL first step in understanding Franklin is to reflect on the difference between him and his contemporary, a great philosopher in a radically different tradition, Jonathan Edwards. Both of these men from youth on had studied and resolved to make use of "the new science" and were influenced especially by the Newtonian scheme. Yet what they made of Newton accentuated the differences between them, rather than uniting them in a common outlook. For Edwards, Newton and Locke provided an armory of new ideas with which to fortify the languishing doctrine of predestination and original sin. He seized on the sensationalistic empiricism of Locke to add a new supernatural sense in order to establish the transcendental truths of revelation and scripture. For Franklin, however, Newtonianism takes its place in the tradition inspired by Francis Bacon, with its emphasis on experimental *knowledge*. It stresses the active, "interfering" aspects of scientific knowing and the human ends which experimental knowledge may come to serve.

Bacon's program issued from dissatisfaction with the barren conceptual dogmatism of neo-Aristotelian and Scholastic learning, and with the high metaphysical Platonism that falsely asserted "that truth is, as it were, the native inhabitant of the human mind and does not come from outside in order to take up its abode there." The more fruitful scientific logic that Bacon recommended, and that Franklin advanced, was some happy match between the mind of man and the nature of things, where *works* would be considered as the test of truth. "Science," Bacon wrote, "must be known by its works. It is by the witness of works rather than by logic or even observation that truth is revealed and established. It follows that the improvement of man's lot and the improvement of man's mind are one and the same thing." In further clarification of Bacon's meaning, one finds in *The Great Instauration* the explicit rejection of "the unkind and ill-starred divorce between the empirical and the rational faculty" and the proposal that they be remarried. From this remarriage should spring "helps to man, and a line and race of inventions that may in some degree subdue and overcome the necessities and miseries of humanity." Therefore, scorn not the "instruments and helps," the technology and craftsmanship once regarded as lowly and intellectually without status: for "neither the bare hand nor the intellect left to itself have much power." This, in drastically compressed form, may be taken to be the Baconian emphasis on experimental naturalism—the philosophy that was reflected in the foundation of the Royal Society and given a new field of influence in America with the establishment of the American Philosophical Society, Franklin's child more than any other's.

We owe to the valuable studies of I. B. Cohen conclusive evidence that Franklin cannot be understood if we take him as an innocent in the scientific family, a naïve inquirer tied to narrow utilitarian pursuits, in the spirit of Max Weber's caricature of him. As Franklin himself indicates time and again, utility is certainly not the immediate object of his concern. Instances abound: at the least, we should bear in mind that it was Franklin who said that philosophy is that which lets light "into the nature of things," and Franklin who founded the Junto and provided its rules, which included the solemn vow, publicly affirmed by each member, to love truth and to seek and serve it. Of greater import, however, is the integral character of his work as a theoretical scientist of the highest order of genius. Only the proper passion for theoretical understanding can explain Franklin's sustained and highly constructive inquiry into the nature of electrical phenomena —an inquiry which might or might not have had ultimate practical significance (although so much the better if the lightning rod *did* come, to protect the lowly everywhere and shelter even the exalted who gathered in St. Paul's cathedral).

What Franklin was able to achieve in his physical inquiry involved the joining of two kinds of activity—the elaboration of theoretical constructs and the elaboration of experimental activity. His conception of electricity as a flow, with negative and positive forces, was a construct that permitted further theoretical developments in the theory of electromagnetism. On the other hand, Franklin's invention of instruments and "helps," such as the lightning rod, bespoke the extensive practical activities of the type that form a valuable part of laboratory work.

1

Here, in Franklin's scientific work and views, we see his pragmatic wisdom in taking theory as a guide to action with the ends in view of both increasing our understanding and improving our lot. But this pragmatic wisdom also appears directly in Franklin's view of morality and politics. His morality, like his science, deliberately cuts free of metaphysics and theology by urging concentration, not on abstract thought or ideal virtue, but on human deeds and their consequences for good or evil. "By their fruits ye shall know them!" Franklin's wisdom in steering clear of the demand for metaphysical or theological agreement or truth, the most elusive of all age-old quests, is shown by his recommendation of procedures that can issue in agreements, concentrating on the increase of agreement by a common method of negotiation to meet common ends. Just as he had come to terms with the rules for establishing empirical truth in other areas, so he proposed workable rules for favoring what he called, with gentle irony, the society of the free-and-easy. Mind the *consequences in experience* of human action, rather than the assumed antecedent metaphysical, theological, or even epistemological premises, is the burden of his enlightened moral advice. Become, he says, not virtuous but a little more virtuous than the day before! Eschewing the Mosaic or Kantian type of imperative, Franklin recommends means to those who would achieve something and implies that the ends of reasonable men cannot but be to "do good."

Franklin also recommends a deliberate imaginative calculation of the expected advantages and disadvantages that would accrue from a voluntary choice—an area indeed where he advances from the traditional humanistic formulation and anticipates the ethics of Bentham—without, however, pretending to model morality on a mathematical or quantifiable basis. In his interesting letter to Joseph Priestley (September 19, 1772), attending to the question of how to determine what to do in difficult cases, he advises marshaling all the considerations pro and con for a contemplated action, setting the reasons pro in one column on a page and the reasons con opposite it. For three or four days enter short hints of the different motives for or against the measure. When they are all set forth in one view, he recommends a qualitative examination of their respective weights. Thus, "If I find a Reason *pro* equal to some Reasons *con*, I strike out the three." What is interesting in the proposal Franklin makes to arrive at a balance of pro over con, or vice versa, is that he appeals throughout to the individual judgment of what is equal, unequal, greater than, or lesser than. At the end he recommends another cooling-off period (a day or two), and then the determination of the question. His final comment is best of all:

And, tho' the Weight of Reasons cannot be taken with the Precision of Algebraic Quantities, yet, when each is thus considered, separately and comparatively, and the whole lies before me, I think I can judge better, and am less liable to make a rash Step; and in fact I have found great Advantage from this kind of Equation, in what may be called *Moral* or *Prudential Algebra.*

We cannot stop to explore the relationship between this letter and Bentham's *Principles of Morals and Legislation,* which was published a few years later, but one major difference should be noted: Franklin never assigns a single source to human action, nor would he be satisfied with the abstract and undifferentiated "masters" of human conduct, pain and pleasure, which Bentham instates as the source of human morality.

2

In groping for more light on the inner dynamism of Franklin's moral philosophy, one should ponder Franklin's early identification of the ideal philosopher as Socrates and the fact that he couples Socrates with the humane Jesus. There is also a striking resemblance between his own artful pattern and the moral ideal of wisdom in the late Renaissance, particularly as expounded in the treatise on wisdom by the Italian mathematician and philosopher, Cardanus. In that work one finds wisdom defined, not as piety nor the virtue achieved by intellectual, metaphysical knowledge, but as a moral virtue, *sapientia naturalis.* Natural wisdom is made synonymous with human happiness and the human goods that result in happiness: tranquillity, modesty, temperance, order, social intercourse, sleep, eating and drinking, and indeed a host of other activities and qualities. The basic formula is that wisdom is the prerequisite to happiness, and virtuous living (and a long life) are the means. The art of virtue is to fight against the evils that man can eliminate by his efforts and to learn to create and hold fast to human goods. There is a Stoic element present in this view of wisdom, so that if the medical and moral precepts do not prove capable of controlling fortune, wisdom as consolation for necessary evils stands ready to perform her office. A prudent wisdom also recognizes the apparently unquenchable hope for immortality, and since it can have no harmful consequences and may function as the cause of a multitude of goods, why not entertain it? As double insurance, however, look to your children and children's children for personal continuation—and beyond that to the most lasting form of immortality, fame. Yet fame for what? Cardanus has his answer: "The longest life is one which has left great, glorious, splendid deeds chronicled in the eternal monuments of history." To live wisely and to survive for a long time, a man must use his precious moments for doing and creating to his fullest measure. Meanwhile, do not eat too much nor drink overly but follow various other familiar rules of both Epicurean and Stoic prescription. Finally, that which most disturbs virtue are the vices of fear, envy, and avarice. Natural wisdom, which begins with shunning vice, flowers into active virtue, which must be acquired through example, reason, meditation, and habitual exercise.

While these are but the skeletal outlines of Cardanus' complex treatise on wisdom, is not the mixture of medicine and ethics to ensure the wise man's art of life uncannily close to Franklin's moral views? That Franklin owns similar beliefs is undeniable; the difference is that the extravagance and profuse vacillations of Cardanus' philosophy are neatly shorn away in Franklin's disciplined garden—all save the cosmic jest lurking in every human resolution to be more perfect. The jest is perhaps but another form of wisdom, the consolation for what man cannot control and cannot perfect, so that the paradox of the human condition and human ill is that certain knowing men will transcend them without visible means and without grace. One version of this view of wisdom is to be found in Franklin's dictum that to be happy even in Paradise requires a happy disposition.

3

As for Franklin's political thought, this presents many puz-
zles and complex questions, partly because one should not
expect a one-to-one correspondence between philosophy and
morality and the region where men are most likely to be
"wolves to one another," but more because of Franklin's apparent disbelief in the value of political theory per se. Since
this is likely to be misunderstood, I hasten to comment that
Franklin cared much about liberty and the dignity of the
common people, and even about "the family of mankind."
But perhaps he felt that theories of the state or of sovereignty
or abstract questions of "who should rule" were somewhat
like those contentious theological arguments that never issued
in resolution but often poisoned the good feeling that might
otherwise have developed as men naturally drew together to
solve urgent, but at least in part manageable, common problems.

In any event, there is a noticeable immediacy about almost
all the Franklin literature devoted to political matters—
whether in his drafting of the Albany Plan of Union, the work
of a far-sighted colonial, or in his Stamp Act performance
before the appraising eyes of Parliament, or in any one of his
potent satirical essays, such as "Rules by Which a Great
Empire May Be Reduced to a Small One." At the American
Enlightenment's particular level of political inspiration—the
definition and formulation of fundamental laws for republican
government and the creation of public statements and determinative policy—Franklin was able and useful but not very
creative, consistent, or detailed in doctrine. Although it is
easy to recognize Franklin's empirical temper in meeting
political questions generally, I think that what is present is
formally describable as experimental humanism and infor-
mally as pragmatic wisdom. For Franklin *is* consistent in maintaining a liberal concern for applied intelligence in every area

where he senses a real issue, as is seen, for instance, in "A Parable against Persecution," or his speeches in the Convention and final comment on the Constitution when the drafting of it was done, or his paper on the slave trade, written and published less than a month before his death. In the concrete analysis of issues that stirred his sympathies and enlisted his particularly civilized brand of reforming zeal, Franklin could not be matched in the America of his day.

A final revealing fact about Franklin's political thought is his activity, the winter before the Constitutional Convention opened, in founding the "Society for Political Enquiries," of which society, as of so many before, he promptly became president. The object of this society was to study political science in the same manner that the American Philosophical Society studied the natural sciences. Franklin was apparently convinced that "the arduous and complicated science of government" had been unprofitably left in the care of practical politicians or confined to the speculations of individual theorists. This transfer of the Baconian experimental scientific approach to the realm of political *inquiry* not only provides the key to his political thought but offers fresh confirmation of his systematic and pervasive commitment to experimental humanism on *all* matters that were live options to him—the philosophy and practice of science, moral theory, wise conduct, and political investigation. It is Franklin, let it be evident, who had named his age the "Age of Experiments" and whose *Autobiography* is a reflection of how integral that concept was to his manner of living. The American experiment was but part of the design, grander and more majestic than the other achievements of his age because, as he saw it, it would perpetuate free society here and, in time, throughout that earth which a philosopher might some day call "my country."

For all these reasons and many more Jefferson called Franklin the "father of American philosophy." The correctness of this appraisal is evident, especially if one reads "American philosophy" to mean that which is creatively and distinctively ours. It is relevant, too, that Jefferson speaks as a part of the eighteenth-century world to which Franklin had given so mighty an impulse, where "philosophy" meant at once the physical sciences and the moral sciences, pursued in the independent secular spirit of experimental and applied intelligence and thus committed to the emancipation of the mind from superstition and prejudice. It is this "philosophy" that Jefferson makes his own, and to this we now turn.

CHAPTER III

Jefferson and the Pursuit of Happiness

JEFFERSON made the pursuit of happiness central to his philosophy of man and society, and in so doing he envisaged a dynamic balance between power and morals. This was aptly summed up by Madison, after the death of his best friend, when he was besieged with requests for inside information about Jefferson. On one such occasion he called attention to the fertility of Jefferson's genius, the vast extent and variety of his acquirements, and "the philosophic impress left on every subject which he touched." But he sensed that he had omitted the essence of that life of spirit and morality which had characterized his dear friend, and so he hastened to add: "Nor was he less distinguished from an early and uniform devotion to the cause of liberty, and systematic preference of a form of Government squared in the strictest degree to the equal rights of man."

There is, therefore, just measure in the appraisal made by the greatest American philosopher of this century, John Dewey, who wrote that Thomas Jefferson was "the first modern to state in human terms the principles of democracy." In claiming for Jefferson the role that Dewey assigns him, there is evidence from Jefferson himself that this, could he achieve it, would be the role he would prefer to anything on earth and under the heavens. For example, sometime around the year 1776 Jefferson, taking notes on Locke's *Letter on Toleration,* had significantly written a comment in an optative mood: "It was a great thing to go so far (as he himself said of the parl. who framed the act of tolern.) but where he stopped short, we may go on."

That Jefferson went on, and America went on, from toleration to religious freedom is very much to the point in our general understanding of the American Enlightenment. It is also arresting to see in this same context Jefferson's understanding of the inadequacy of isolating even so basic a value as toleration and converting it to an absolute and potentially fanatical ideal, adherence to which may bring the destruction of self and society. For he also comments on specific measures of toleration, that civil offenses should be punished, but that in the absence of civil offense, it should suffice that "the other opinions may be despised." One exception Jefferson makes, however, that bears serious thought. He writes: "Perhaps the single thing which may be required to others before toleration to them would be an oath that they would allow toleration to others." He is recommending, of course, that we accept the rules for free society and uncoerced belief, and he is cognizant of the moral stupidity of assuming that those who would annihilate the rules that make political and social freedom possible should be tolerated by the men whose freedom would be lost by so absolute and unintelligent an elevation of the principle of toleration beyond all calculation of human consequences and cost.

Flexibility, patience, and the prudent weighing of alternatives in the light of the consequences of choice are roughly characteristic of a pragmatic liberal temper, although not of doctrinaire liberalism. Jefferson's democratic philosophy is fine-grained and pure in its principles but sanctions no abrogation of reason and moral prudence; in short, it sees no opportunity for moral holidays in the name of absolute idealism or absolute daemonism. Thus, he is convinced that only governments that are constitutional and limited in power by their willingness to yield to the voice and rights of the people can ever be compatible with the full measure of human dignity and responsibility which he considered it his own greatest cause to protect and further.

1

In the light of this belief, it may be useful to consider again what Jefferson intended in drafting the Declaration of Independence, which he wrote at almost the same time he wrote his comment on Locke. It is in that guiding philosophical document that America's explicit attachment to free society is pronounced before a "candid world"—a pronouncement effective even today, when the world has perhaps lost a little of her candid luster. The basic propositions of the Declaration concerned the rights of man, and I should therefore like to call attention to Jefferson's language as he first wrote it, in order to make his meaning clearer. "We hold these truths to be sacred and undeniable; that all men are created equal and independent, that from that equal creation they derive rights inherent and inalienable, among which are the preservation of life, liberty, and the pursuit of happiness."

It is a matter of great consequence to notice that Jefferson's first try at formulating this basic assumption about human nature and society refers to "sacred and undeniable" truths. These original terms are value-freighted, emotional terms— as they should be. For Jefferson was not engaged purely in the construction of scientific theory in this moving human document. He was writing an American manifesto to mobilize the thirteen colonies for a war of independence and to win for them the sentiment of the civilized world. For this purpose he was evolving the moral ends by which free men would like to live; he was attempting to lay down the fundamental ideals by which all free societies should conduct public affairs. These are value preferences, as Jefferson said; they are "sacred," if you hold them as strongly as he did.

It is worthwhile to call attention to the original language, "sacred and undeniable," because the final wording, "self-evident," has been subjected to a battery of attack from Jefferson's time on. The implication the attack carries is dangerous, since by rejecting the thesis that there can be significant self-evident knowledge, one appears to undermine the valuable human rights that are adduced as prime illustrations thereof.

The "sacred" truth which is taken as fundamental by Jefferson is the equality of man. Now, since the principle of equality is at the heart of the philosophy of the Declaration but has come to mean many things, it is essential to decide what Jefferson meant by it. He did not mean an arithmetical equality, which reduces all men to the same level of talent, ability, moral discipline, or practical genius. On the contrary, Jefferson wrote with conviction about the existence of "a natural aristocracy." This approaches the paradox posed by George Orwell in his *Animal Farm:* "All animals are equal; but some are more equal than others." Just how much inequality can there be without abandoning the idea of equality? But Jefferson was not describing a fact about the actual biological, personal, or social conditions of men. He was describing a fact about the essential traits of the species—that there is a human nature and that this human nature is the same in all men. And he was prescribing a policy that would allow men to realize their nature as fully as possible. The principle of equality, so understood, asserts that man is more than a mere parcel of matter and more than an animal. He is a person who has intelligence and needs society. In sum, Jefferson affirmed that if men are treated as valuable human beings, they are likely to fulfill their potential more completely than if they are treated otherwise.

The famous triad of rights, "life, liberty and the pursuit of happiness," is, as Jefferson said, derived from the equality of man's nature. They are "inherent and inalienable" because natural to man. The right to life is the right of a person to existence. The right to liberty is the right of a person to conduct his life as master of himself and his acts. But what about the right to the "pursuit of happiness"? Recent scholars have worked on this phrase, without, however, doing much to illuminate its meaning. They were content to point out that John Locke, in his *Second Treatise on Civil Government,* had named "life, liberty and property" as the basic natural rights. Then, in a somewhat imaginative way, they immediately assumed that Jefferson's borrowed context had been immediately and precisely the Lockean triad of rights. Consequently there was only one significant change to explain—the substitution of "the pursuit of happiness" for Locke's "property." What they made of this was explicitly or derivatively influenced by Marx's economic-determinist view of history. Locke was declared to be a narrow bourgeois, writing in defense of the propertied classes; whereas Jefferson was a revolutionist, encouraged by his temporary radicalism to voice a hope that encompassed propertied and unpropertied people alike. Parrington, for example, considers that the change "marks a complete break with the Whiggist doctrine of property rights that Locke had bequeathed to the English middle class." And there is the correlative view, which owes much to Beard, that the Constitution involved a break with the Declaration of Independence, because of its built-in protection of property rights.

The facts are: Jefferson did know and did admire the work of John Locke, and he agreed with him that there is a natural right to property. For Locke speaks of property as the inclusive term for all that a person possesses, including his faculties, his ability to labor, and his health. The right to property relates to the human being as an extension of himself. Thus, Locke wrote that "God, who hath given the world to men in common, hath also given them reason to make use of it. . . . The earth and all that is therein is given to men for the support and comfort of their being." This right to property enables Jefferson to criticize specific property laws where these pervert natural rights and fail to serve the common good. In justifying this claim, Jefferson used a formula reminiscent of that of John Locke: "The earth is given as a common stock for man to labor and live on." In summing up this belief he wrote that "the true foundation of republican government . . . is the equal right of every citizen, in his person and property."

Now, if Jefferson subscribed to the Lockean triad of natural rights, why did he leave out the mention of property? The practical reasons are clear. Jefferson wanted eloquent symbols in his democratic manifesto, and stylistic sensibility alone might have made him prefer the phrase "the pursuit of happiness" over the uninspiring and legalistic term "property." And sense strongly reinforced sound. Jefferson knew that the country would soon be asking loyal support of those without property as well as those with it, just as he knew that American Tories, who had refused to join the patriot ranks, might have their property confiscated. Still more sensible was his concern to avoid an appeal to property on the eve of the repudiation of Great Britain's complicated claims that the colonies, founded on the basis of royal grants in many cases, were and should remain her property.

2

It might still be argued that, although Locke and Jefferson agree on the natural right to property, Jefferson was going beyond Locke in his advocacy of the right to the pursuit of happiness. But Locke and Jefferson appear to be in complete accord on the pursuit of happiness too. Indeed, Locke provided a most searching analysis of the right to the pursuit of happiness in his *Essay Concerning Human Understanding*, which seems to have left its impress on Jefferson. This is indicated by the extraordinarily high valuation Jefferson placed on Locke as a moral philosopher. Some dozen years after the Declaration he went to considerable trouble to obtain portraits of "the three greatest men that ever lived, without any exception"—Bacon, Newton, and Locke. Jefferson ceaselessly admired Locke, who, in his masterpiece, had broken new paths toward understanding the power of empirical knowledge. The *Essay* was widely read in the Colonies prior to the Declaration —and it would be strange indeed if the Puritan, Jonathan Edwards, would react to Locke's works like a miser to the discovery of boundless gold, whereas, a half-century later, Jefferson, despite his humanistic spirit and extensive reading, would confine himself to the thin slice of Locke's political writings. More circumstantial details support the hypothesis that Jefferson knew the *Essay* before 1776. He was one of the outstanding students at William and Mary College—a college founded by Dr. James Blair, who corresponded with Locke and probably had presentation copies of Locke's major works. These copies must have been in existence at the time Jefferson used the college library; and many other libraries of close friends, especially that of Dabney Carr, Jefferson's alter ego, contained Locke's *Essay*.

These iffy conjectures may give the far-off scent of scholarly battle; but something of prime importance is our reward. In Locke's chapter on "Power," there are numerous references to the pursuit of happiness, precisely in those words. But the great significance of turning to this text of Locke's is not simply the repeated use of the exact phrase but the insistent theme they underline—*that personal power and morals are necessarily conjoined in man as a species, as a human being.*

The heart of the moral philosophy that Locke is proposing in this chapter is its view of liberty. Liberty is the power to act or to forbear acting. A man is free insofar as he has the power to think or not to think, to move or not to move, according to the preference of his own mind. What is the relation between man's freedom and happiness? "Happiness," he firmly declares, "everyone constantly pursues, and desires what makes any part of it." But some who are constant in pursuit of happiness do not have a clear view of "good, great and confessed good." "The mind [has] . . . a power to suspend the execution and satisfaction of any of its desires, and . . . is at liberty to consider the objects of them, examine them on all sides, and weigh them with others." When this liberty is not used rightly, we make the mistakes which ruin that happiness we naturally seek. "As . . . the highest perfection of intellectual nature lies in a careful and constant pursuit of true and solid happiness, so the care of ourselves, that we mistake not imaginary for real happiness, is the necessary foundation of our liberty."

The theory of the good advanced by Locke and accepted by Jefferson is that what is good for man can be determined from his nature. The good is a refinement and reconsideration of the natural promptings of the needs for satisfaction and security. Thus we are not dealing with any form of raw or crude hedonism nor with an unmitigated rationalism. We are, rather, involved in humanistic or deliberative naturalism. The desired is nowhere confused with the desirable. Only what is desirable is a moral value, and only what is desirable *ought* to be desired, and ought to be pursued. What, however, distinguishes the desirable from the desired? Basically, the desirable is that which contributes to real and substantial happiness—and this is an empirical judgment. When knowledge guides our will, and choices are made after we have examined the good or evil of what we desire, we are at once free and on the road to true happiness.

Locke and Jefferson are, of course, aware that men have come to pursue different courses, even though all men desire happiness. The two chief explanations for this are that men fail to take thought and thus mistake the good and, secondly, that the same thing is not good to every man alike. Self-realization and awareness of the variety among personalities are cardinal values for personal and social morality. The first value, self-realization, stresses the right of the human being to live his own life. The second value, awareness of individual variety, protects us from a dead-level uniformity and welcomes a plurality of personal selves.

These are some of the focal points in a discussion of life, liberty, and the pursuit of happiness for a student of Locke. The life of man consists of the use of the powers associated with his mind. These form his understanding, which distinguishes him from all other sensible creatures, as Locke pointedly states in the very first sentence of the *Essay:* "It is the *understanding* that sets men above the rest of sensible beings, and gives him all the advantage and dominion which he has over them." Thus Locke's basic definition of liberty connects man's life of reason with freedom to employ it. The absence of freedom is necessity or tyranny. Jefferson's famous statement in the first year of the nineteenth century comes to mind: "I have sworn upon the altar of God, eternal hostility against every form of tyranny over the mind of man." The life of reason involves the free use of the mind to pursue happiness and overcome uneasiness of mind or body—it is the life fitting for man, in view of the natural capacities of human nature. This is Locke's moral philosophy, and it is helpful to recall that Locke is the only moral philosopher in Jefferson's trinity of the greatest men.

3

We have seen that the right to the pursuit of happiness consists of the right to the pursuit, not of material advantages, but of the life of reason and the fulfillment of the human nature. Now, what did Jefferson conceive that happiness to be, in more concrete and personal terms? In accounting for the richness of Jefferson's conception of happiness, one must add the strong influence of the Greek and Roman classics to that of Locke. As an intensive classical scholar he was not only familiar with the Stoics and Epicureans but prized their work above that of any other ancient philosophers. This earlier tradition, as Jefferson often said, was rich with integrative ideals of human happiness; what impressed him in it was the blending of happiness and virtue. Such a view of private happiness is hostile to the doctrine that human happiness is self-centered, narrowly self-interested. On this ground Jefferson offered an incisive criticism of Hobbesian egoism and took issue with the attitude of Helvetius that self-love is the root of even our seemingly altruistic behavior. Jefferson's objections were drawn from his view of man as a social creature rather than from the isolated individual that some eighteenth-century theorists envisaged.

But *how* can virtue be a guide to the pursuit of happiness? Jefferson's answer here moved beyond the ancient philosopers to the inspiration of Jesus, for he considered that the ancients failed to recognize the reality of love and of duties toward others. Jefferson went to considerable trouble twice in his life to collect "The Life and Morals of Jesus of Nazareth" from the books of the New Testament. He believed it was Jesus who had set the Western world on a more humane moral level by teaching "the most sublime and benevolent code of morals which has ever been offered to man." In the original Christian ethic Jefferson saw two correctives to the selfishness of the ancients and the sophisticated selfishness of some moderns. He emphasized inward motive and intention as well as the outward act and its consequences. And he accepted with full readiness the spirit of benevolence, charity, and love of one's fellow men that begins with one's family and reaches to one's friends and neighbors and, in some measure (naturally diluted in terms of intensity of feeling), to "the whole human family."

Jefferson's view of Jesus as a humane rather than a divine person is given further support by Jefferson's avowed humanism and his sympathy with the humanistic-skeptical tradition of Pierre Charron. Because of the neglect of Charron and his importance in Jefferson's moral philosophy, I shall briefly consider his work *De la Sagesse.* Jefferson admired that work profoundly. When George Ticknor visited Jefferson at Monticello, in 1815, they conversed of many things, practical and urgent, philosophical, moral, and political, and Ticknor then recorded in his journal that Mr. Jefferson told him that he thought Charron's *De la Sagesse* the best treatise on moral philosophy ever written.

Charron's work has been called "the philosophical *Summa* of humanism at the end of the sixteenth century." It is explicitly secular in emphasis, making wisdom purely human and typically manifest in action rather than in contemplation, in virtue rather than in knowledge as such. A strong critique of the speculative traditions of wisdom—from the idea of wisdom as the perfect knowledge of divine and human things to first principles and metaphysics—voices the complaint that they commit men to no action and nothing useful, but encourage flight from the world and the society of other men. Wisdom, for Charron, should commit men to the world, should be *human,* aiming, through the union of action and contemplation, at beauty and nobility of character in the whole man. The dignity of man, the "excellence and perfection of man as man," are based on an ethic that issues in the ancient virtues of prudence, justice, fortitude, and temperance. If knowledge does not function to make our lives happier, it is a "small and sterile good" and may, on occasion, be even worse than that. Wisdom must be active, ready to control and govern things. In general, Charron's attack on pedantry leads him to a sharp distinction between moral wisdom and knowledge and to a skeptical distrust of the potency of man's purely rational faculties. He steers clear of the extreme of Pyrrhonist skepticism through his belief that men, who cannot know the truth with certainty, can nevertheless distinguish good from evil and can choose and effect the one and reject the other.

Jefferson did not stress the skeptical attack on man's rational powers, although he too believed in the union of will and intellect, head and heart, and the identification of virtue with the whole man committed in action to himself, his neighbors, and the public world. But the implication which Charron drew from his account of wisdom, that its first component must be a "universal, full, entire, generous and seigneurial intellectual freedom," was Jefferson's most cherished ideal. Equally arresting by way of comparison between Charron's ideal of wisdom and Jefferson's, are the command to follow nature and the idea that nature is clearly demarcated from the supernatural. The captive intellects that submit to revelation cannot follow nature in the wise man's way. Man is good, virtuous, just, because his reason, his nature, as part of the larger context of nature, demands such habits and conduct. To live well and die well is a human quest—undertaken by reason, which is natural to man—and part of nature in its most extensive scope. Charron's moral position, like Jefferson's, is thus naturalistic and humanistic.

4

On more personal grounds still, how did Jefferson envisage happiness for himself? By his own testimony the delight of life began with his own family circle. Nothing caused him more regret than the loss of privacy that public duties often demanded of him. Not one to lament, Jefferson more nearly laments this deprivation than any other in his long life. And the extraordinary love and loyalty he cherished for his wife, Martha, which determined him to live the second half of his life as a widower, has been testified to in many interesting ways and from many divergent sources. It is fairly well known that Jefferson brought his two daughters to Paris at considerable trouble to himself—he could not bear to be parted from them too long. If anything, the record shows Jefferson as an anxious, too-loving father and his daughters as loyal, too-affectionate daughters. But we are not interested in psychoanalysis at this point. We are only identifying what was essential in Jefferson's private horizon of happiness, and love and family life were by all signs first.

The testimony of a long life is impressive. By that testimony we know that Jefferson's personal happiness depended vitally upon the enduring ties of friendship. When Jefferson had experienced the rigors of political life, he meditated upon the gratifications of friendship and wrote: "Agreeable society is the first essential in constituting the happiness, and, of course, the value of our existence." The extent, depth, and duration of his friendships were fabulous, and this spirit shines through his vast correspondence. No one could feel more painfully the separation or the loss of friends—as is evidenced by the ardor with which Jefferson re-opened his connection with John Adams. On that occasion he wrote, "I find friendship to be like wine, raw when new, ripened with age, the true old man's milk and restorative cordial." But nothing in political history seems more like a perpetual miracle than the fifty-year-long affectionate and cordial collaboration between Jefferson and Madison.

Cumulative testimony also demonstrates his love for knowledge as an inherent delight and as a condition for man's freedom. His early work for the diffusion of knowledge was only the beginning of a lifetime's devotion to the improvement of education—an education which he fully understood in humanistic terms as self-justifying but which he passionately wished to see at the service of free men and enlightened governments. Unlike many professional educators, there was no level of education that was below or beyond Jefferson's concern— primary, secondary, collegiate, advanced research of a sort we call "postgraduate" today, or adult education. In the closing years of his life, Jefferson labored to build, on the basis of his dream and a collection of blueprints, a real, functioning university—the University of Virginia. He said he wanted the University to be dedicated to the illimitable freedom of the human mind, and he pored over his books and book catalogues to work out library lists for it, he raised funds to build it, he worked out detailed curriculums for it, and he personally carried on a fatiguing battle to recruit the best European and American staff an infant university could command.

Occupation he found not only essential to health but to happiness. Rising at five in the morning and making each day an acquisition—by unsparing work, an extensive correspondence on a genuinely philosophical level, and perpetual service to his country and to his ever-widening community of friends and coworkers in the realm of knowledge—was perhaps a recipe for fatigue but never for ennui. Jefferson's versatility has been much admired and regarded as a triumph of talent and fortune. Admittedly it was that, but it was talent and fortune cultivated, disciplined, even relentlessly pursued, in the wise manner of one who has learned that happiness eludes those who expect to seize it directly, without the interposition of objective interests that, being objective, require knowledge, care, and labor to make them strong.

To the happiness of loving and being loved, pursuing wisdom through knowledge, and engaging in all-absorbing activities, he added uprightness of mind, a clear conscience, and the benevolence that transcends justice in human relations. On these Jefferson placed more than instrumental value; he spoke like an old Stoic when enjoining such virtues on the young who solicited his advice (although his tender affection could not long be suppressed and would end by softening the rigors of the sound advice he meant to impart). They were not empty or merely verbal allegiances but active principles of life for this unique statesman.

5

We have taken a brief look at Jefferson's notion of the "pursuit of happiness" as it operated in his private life. I believe that there is no need for the usual apologies in pausing for biographical material in the course of a scrutiny of philosophic ideas, for Jefferson too placed the individual man first in his philosophy and framed his social theory in the light of the moral nature of the human being. Man is "destined," Jefferson said, for society. Since it is part of man's nature to want society, he institutes it, not to rule over him as if he were a slave or a child, but to provide justice. Man retains his rights to regulate society jointly with "all those who have concurred in its procurement." Whenever society loses its limited character as an instrument designed by human beings to advance the human purposes of freedom, fellowship, and justice and arrogates to itself the power to crush the "inherent and inlienable rights of man," at that juncture society should be resisted. For although the individual will accept many limitations upon his freedom in the light of social duties and obligations that reflection shows him are necessary or wise, he cannot compromise his claim to be considered an "end" in and by society, never only a "means." Jefferson makes the human being, in his pursuit of true and substantial happiness, the governing ideal for moral and social theory.

Jefferson's philosophy of human nature thus supports his personal vista of what the pursuit of happiness is like. But it has an even deeper significance for the relationship between power and morals in his system of beliefs. Contemporary theories of personality have made us all familiar with the idea of man as an interpersonal being, characterized by the capacity and need for both intelligence and love. Even psychoanalytic theory envisions the mature, aware, self-realizing person as the one for whom the pursuit of happiness is an open avenue, not a fatal cul-de-sac as it is for the neurotic, the mentally sick. Without benefit of extensive empirical findings, Jefferson seemed to comprehend these thoughts fully. Indeed, Jefferson himself is a beautiful embodiment of the mature, integrated, and open personality.

Perhaps this was the real secret of Jefferson's political influence. One value derived from consulting his encyclopedic correspondence and papers is the emergence of Jefferson "in the round"—the full man, revealed not only in the myriad letters to friends and acquaintances but in their letters to him as well. We are fond, today, of employing the term "charismatic" leader, although the circumstances of the modern world tend to connect such leadership with anything but mental health, stability, and virtue. Jefferson affords the rare contrast—he is the model of the natural and compelling leader whose moral character and enlightened mind wins him followers, quite without deliberate strategy or design. This is what Jefferson meant to many in his own day and helps to explain his continuing hold over the American imagination in our own times and doubtless for future times as well. Does this not amount, then, to the power of moral ideals and example? And is this not the most durable, the most "human," and ultimately the strongest power over man as an individual? In this setting, of course, power becomes something like authority—that natural form of authority that derives from rational and moral sources.

In social terms, the import of the foregoing remarks is this: that society is most perfect that promotes the tendencies toward integration. And integration must be understood as twofold: as a property of individual personalities and as a social relationship among persons who accept the principles of consent, joint deliberation, mutual concern, sympathy, and determined action for the improvement of social institutions. Thus, for society, the primacy of the human being implies the controlling ideal of the common good. This is the view that moved Jefferson to assert that governments are formed for the happiness of man. In the final analysis, then, there is a unity about Jefferson as a private and as a public person. His personal life and his political life were on good speaking terms, and what we can learn from either aspect helps to illuminate the pattern of the other.

6

As we have already seen in our discussion of Locke's theory of happiness based on human choice, a society that respects individuals encourages their freedom to choose in its political setting. The external marks of a political environment encouraging to human freedom are government by consent of the people; periodic elections to choose new representatives or continue old ones in power for limited periods of time; freedom to speak and publish one's criticisms of political policies; and the right to public information about the conduct of government business. Jefferson thought that, because mystery and secrecy were extensively employed by governments that ruled over the people, publicity and openness to inquiry should be extensively employed by governments that represent the people. These of course are directional trends in two different types of government, not absolute criteria.

Underlying these concrete expressions of man's power to choose is the faith that man can benefit by education, that he can learn to participate in the business of self-government, if with difficulty and with a tolerable margin of error. Jefferson did not believe, as he is sometimes naïvely assumed to have believed, that the people are normally, naturally, and for the most part "wise" and thus ready agents of democratic government! As Jefferson himself defined this particular issue, he asserted his trust in the people in this explicit sense: that they were to be cherished and considered as "the most honest and safe, although not the most wise depository of the public interests." He contrasted the democratic trust in the people with the aristocratic distrust of them, which wishes "to draw all powers from them into the hands of the higher classes." Whom and what did one fear more? The ignorance of the people? Or the selfishness of rulers independent of them? Jefferson, of course, took the latter as the overriding danger. But he went further than this. He thought that the role of power in society involved a basic question: Is there a power independent of right? Jefferson's uncompromising answer to this is: "There exists a right independent of force." He was determined that this right should limit force in a democratic state. He did not say that, since there is a right independent of force, right will triumph tomorrow, or we will see it vindicated of a certainty within the span of a given generation. But he did believe that when states neglected right, when they mounted the tiger with runaway power, their abuse of human rights and the evils of their "Egyptian oppression," would prove intolerable to the common humanity of their victims.

As part of his faith Jefferson found a special mission for democratic society, based as it was upon the rights of the people to participate in self-government. This was to remind the oppressed that there were sanctuaries for those who were misruled, that man could still seek happiness in other climes. "A single good government," Jefferson wrote, "becomes thus a blessing to the whole earth."

Force, as Jefferson knew, if not checked in society, "ends necessarily in military despotism," in tyranny. It is for this reason that even those who speak of order and yet fear the people must be contained. But what do we turn to as a fundamental limit on force? The law of the majority as the prime and sacred law of every society of individuals of equal rights, Jefferson replies. Once this law is disregarded, whether in the name of a minority of "better" or "wiser" or "more substantial" citizens, we are landsliding into a servile state, preparing for the will of a self-selected "advance" guard of the community to impose itself on the subject people.

For Jefferson this recognition of the moral value of the people and the sacred law of the majority which implements that recognition are even more fundamental than a written constitution. It was no part of Jefferson's hope for a progressive betterment of society to bind future generations to the specific level of wisdom and knowledge of means of an earlier generation. Believing in the reality of human error and in the partial, rather than total, grasp of truth, Jefferson thought it essential to leave open the roads to further experimentation by the co-operative efforts of inquiring minds. His famous dictum that "the earth belongs to the living" is a comment on constitutions and so-called fundamental laws, and in one phrase suggests the attitude that he elsewhere makes explicit when he speaks of the revered American Constitution. It is well known that when Jefferson, the American Ambassador in

France, received copies of the Constitution from the several friends who had played a role in the Convention, he scanned it anxiously and thoughtfully and came up with the criticism that there had been no explicit provision to safeguard the rights of the people. "The absence of express declarations ensuring freedom of religion, freedom of the press, freedom of the person under the uninterrupted protection of the Habeas corpus, and trial by jury in Civil as well as in Criminal cases, excited my jealousy," he wrote. And he did not let his argument rest until it had found zealous advocates in some of his friends who actively supported the fight for a Bill of Rights in the state legislatures. As Jefferson saw the change from the Confederation to the federated Republic, it was a victory for stronger government, and "our government wanted bracing." But it must not be braced too high, and in the context of the new framework Jefferson confessed that his most formidable dread was "the tyranny of the legislatures." It was a great victory of principle, in Jefferson's view, when "the rights which it is useless to surrender to the government, and which governments have yet always been found to invade" were specifically protected by the addition of the first ten amendments to the new constitution.

In human terms the Bill of Rights implies that the people of a free society are to pursue happiness suitably to their diverse personalities, their perhaps heretical opinions and beliefs, and their eccentricities. Men free to inquire and free to express their beliefs and judgments could coexist only in the embracive tolerance of social pluralism. Such a society would unquestionably be rich in disagreement, sometimes rife with controversy, occasionally bitter with conflict. But it would be a society devoted to the dignity of man, one that refuses to stamp out the differences among men. Truth might not always prevail in such a world, but reasonable men would remain free to explore the evidence and marshal the arguments in her defense. Two conditions could limit the open generosity of this environment without necessarily deserting this fundamental ideal: the grave crisis of wartime when free men must work for defense of their country and the fight against a conspiracy that masquerades as heresy. (A conspiracy, as opposed to a heresy, organizes, to employ force ruthlessly and relentlessly against a society that abjures the use of violence as a method for achieving legitimate governmental power.)

Yet, as he develops his argument with Madison it is Jefferson who calls attention to the fact that the Bill of Rights must be looked on as *general rules* to preserve as much freedom under government as possible. He admits that in some cases the rules will be abused or will themselves be defective, but comments: "The few cases wherein these things may do evil, cannot be weighed against the multitude wherein the want of them will do evil." He considers several illustrations —in each case weighing the moral advantages of having a general rule about freedom of speech and press, for example, against the disadvantages that flow from abuse of these freedoms. He concludes: "My idea then is, that tho' proper exceptions to these general rules are desirable and probably practicable, yet if the exceptions cannot be agreed on, the establishment of the rules in all cases will do ill in very few."

7

This is not the voice of absolute idealism or doctrinaire liberalism but the voice of cautious, deliberative, and reasonable pragmatic wisdom. With some amusement, in his old age Jefferson would say of the American experiment and the faith that sustained it: "We shall have our follies without doubt. . . . But ours will be the follies of enthusiasm, not of bigotry." Man must choose, and never under the fully free conditions he would like, never out of the circle of competing and plural evils and goods. The enthusiasm that would permit one to steer a perilous course for human freedom is the alternative Jefferson will always be identified with, as his historic role. For he knew clearly, in this treacherous world, the face of moral and political evil, however much he would grope for the foundations of what was good. He would make pragmatic use of his "enthusiasm" to avoid a society where men would be reduced to "mere automatons of misery . . . [with] no sensibilities left but for sinning and suffering." For that is the beginning, he said, of "the *bellum omnium in omnia,* which some philosophers observing to be so general in this world, have mistaken it for the natural, instead of the abusive state of man." The abusive state of man he kept in mind throughout complex constitutional and legal questions and in every advance he proposed in the rules, the education, and the moral climate of free society.

In an almost elliptical phrase in an 1819 letter to John Adams, Jefferson reveals that he has taken the measure of the significance of American democratic thought and its public issue when he writes: "I see with pride that as we are ahead of Europe in Political science, so on other subjects we are getting along side of them." There is no better way to define the American Enlightenment than to see where it had concentrated its strongest drive and what, on balance, its own leaders considered it had achieved. The conclusion is as simple as Jefferson makes it: "We are ahead of Europe in Political science!" Ahead because only in the American Enlightenment had liberty not been opposed to equality, but the double and complementary values of both had been publicly affirmed and to a promising degree publicly acted upon or "backed up." Men like Jefferson and Madison and John Adams were steeped in the knowledge of history from classical times to their own day, learned in the history of law and constitutional government, and realistic about the dangerous trade of democracy as they established the essential political liberties which would permit further development of democratic society. This might be taken in another sense as meaning that while they stanchly defended the principle of majority rule, they did not make a mystique of the unitary will of the nation out of it. This was a further proof of their prudent use of experience and their wisdom about the right to dissent, to criticize, to air differences, and, in short, to practice the privileges of intellectual freedom. If the obligation of self-government meant an educated and alert citizenry, it meant something very exacting about the leaders of such a system too: wisdom without fanaticism, belief and conviction and even imagination without authoritarian and elitist presumptions, and the unremitting labor of facing issues one by one, so that reform, while notably successful and on many levels, was not pushed by intemperate and hasty zealots bent upon "wiping the slate clean" or ignoring the profound importance of timing.

Jefferson's moral philosophy is very much to the point in considering why he entered and stayed in politics, why he was quite ready to leave it without a backward glance, and why he used his power and influence in the direction that he did. For Jefferson's humanism, his benevolence, his respect for the individual and the unknown capacities for growth and achievement that every young generation would have, relate to his political measures in a fundamental way. As we have seen, there is a substantial correlation between his private and fundamentally moral conception of individual happiness and his political ideals as crystallized in the phrase "the pursuit of happiness."

8

This brings us to the crucial issue of the relationship between power and morals in Jefferson's philosophy. We have seen that under the directive ideal of the common right of all to pursue happiness, Jefferson curbed state power by the moral demand for justice and the continuing control of the people's choice. In the familiar language of Jefferson's day, the natural rights of man were derived from or connected with natural law. He affirmed the rights of man on a preponderantly moral basis of preference and appropriateness to human nature. Self-realization, always in the interpersonal context of other selves, may be the natural moral goal. On this basis, the heart and the head can both speak, one in terms of normal good feeling, the other in terms of normal good sense, in behalf of natural rights. Natural law, in this interpretation, is the system of governing norms, rules, and duties that bind man—the correlative, in short, of the natural rights which he claims. Natural law in its widest legalistic sense (what Jefferson invariably referred to as "the law of nature and nations") includes this meaning plus the usages and customs of nations dealing with other nations in the interest of peace and under the controlling ideal of more humane and civilized practice. In this view, one finds oneself directed to the great enduring moral principles—the worth of every human being, the consequent equality of consideration to which all are entitled in society, justice, and fraternity. And these overarching moral ideals are in no way limited to a given time or society but invoke the vision of a brotherhood of man.

The important consequence is that one hereby asserts a moral limit on power politics; one condemns force and violence as an extensive, wholesale instrument of national or international policy. This limit Jefferson enthusiastically advocated. He nourished the hope that just as men had been able to fashion a society substituting peaceful discussion and popular decision for force and fear, so nations in time would work out a pattern on somewhat the same moral lines of long-range mutual interest. His vigorous rejection of the theory that regards man as a narrowly selfish creature, psychologically motivated only and always by his own exclusive interest, is paralleled by his rejection of naked power politics on the level of international affairs. Jefferson saw that the same moral laws that "the Author of Nature" had established between man and man apply to nation and nation. When these laws—of peace, friendship, honesty, and reasonable negotiation of conflicts—are defied, nations return to the "depths of human enormity" that Jefferson often identified with the era of the Borgias, the low point of national morality from which he saw a gradual advance to his own day, a movement "softening and correcting the manners and morals of man." Having witnessed in the eighteenth century the growth of science and the arts, enlightened public opinion, and the increased dignity and distinction of character of great nations, Jefferson was appalled at the abandonment of moral restraints. He thought such behavior not only immoral but self-defeating in the longer run. "Had Bonaparte reflected that such is the moral construction of the world, that no national crime passes unpunished in the long run, he would not now be in the cage of St. Helena."

But in the modern world great tyrants and murderous despots can die quietly in bed if we can trust to the ministrations and reports of their doctors. Apparently the "moral construction of the world" has not caged all the enemies of mankind nor punished those who incarnated the powers of darkness and evil. To this hard fact which saps the courage of the timid, Jefferson replied: There will be penalties for wrongs done to one's country or other countries; they cannot slip by without the inevitable payment made for oppression. "The seeds of hatred and revenge which present oppressors are now sowing with a large hand, will not fail to produce their fruits in time. Like their brother robbers on the highway, they suppose the escape of the moment a final escape, and deem infamy and future risk countervailed by present gain." But Jefferson believed, of course, that they suppose wrong. The individual cannibal may escape, but the legacy of cannibalism is a ravaged country and, in time, disintegration, internal warfare, and rivers of blood. In the long run, then, the morality that respects human nature and reason as the umpire of conflict in society is the only reliable guide to national self-interest. "No nation, however powerful," he wrote to Madison, "any more than an individual, can be unjust with impunity. Sooner or later public opinion, an instrument merely moral in the beginning, will find occasion physically to inflict its sentence on the unjust."

It might be natural to raise the question whether Jefferson's strong belief in peace and in the rights of man implied a general position of pacifism. We shall let this realistic idealist answer for himself: "The love of peace which we sincerely feel and profess," he wrote, "has begun to produce an opinion in Europe that our government is entirely in Quaker principles and will turn the left cheek when the right has been smitten. This opinion must be corrected when just occasion arises, or we shall become the plunder of all nations." Jefferson's life spanned two very different epochs in the political development of the modern world—the hopeful remission of corrupt monarchy and the growth of revolutionary movements, led by the American Revolution, in the eighteenth century, and the Napoleonic wars, the mighty battle of lions and tigers, which opened the nineteenth century. What Jefferson called the "daring profligacy and avowed destitution of all moral principle" in this era, sickened his soul unto death. But in a world that substituted the rule of force for the rule of law, where predatory despots were desolating mankind, Jefferson thought war preferable to and less ruinous than peace.

9

Those who insist upon reducing Jefferson to a flat line-drawing of the visionary idealist prefer to explain away these various elements in his position on power and morals by charging him with inconsistency or hypocrisy. I must confess that such views seem absurd to me. They express the irritation of those who oversimplify values, who wish to force an absolutist position—even upon men who make it explicit that for them the actual consequences of any value for the lives and welfare of human beings determine its weight in competition with alternative values. Indeed, Jefferson's most revealing characterization of his philosophy of power breathes eternal defiance to the either-or, one-and-only-one species of mankind. Epitomizing the ideal of American democratic government, Jefferson referred to it as an "empire for liberty." He thus joins in lifelike tension two compelling concepts, one symbolizing strength for self-preservation and growth, the other indicating the object for which that national strength, that power to resist outside manipulation and aggression, is to be sought: so that freedom, under the kind of benign government that values men and respects their natural rights, can be realized in fact.

It is significant that Jefferson first began to use the term "empire for liberty" after the acquisition of Louisiana—when he had already decided that real national power was essential for survival in a world where aggressive and unscrupulous great powers were carving out their empires in bloody battle. In 1803 Jefferson used the phrase calling attention to the fact that Louisiana added to the nation gave America security from foreign intrigues and opened "a noble prospect . . . for ages. . . . The world will here see such an extent of country under a free and moderate government as it has never yet seen." In 1805 he stressed the importance of this new source of strength as an addition to "the great republican family of this hemisphere" and exulted that it would secure "the blessings of civil and religious freedom to millions yet unborn." And, with majestic enthusiasm, Jefferson wrote to his great friend Madison, as the latter received the President's mantle, that the world might soon see a unique spectacle in the West—a democratic country that had achieved strength and power without betraying the liberal and humane principles that had inspired it since the first crisis of its birth as a nation. If so, he wrote, "we should have such an empire for liberty as the world has never surveyed since the creation; and I am persuaded no constitution was ever before so well calculated as ours for extensive empire and self-government."

The empire for liberty, after all, rested upon self-government. It was in this sense that Jefferson was once moved to say that "the last hope of human liberty in this world rests on us"—and he was not sure that we would advance in that political wisdom and virtue, that loyalty to the high morality of self-government, required in a vexed and turmoiled world. But he rested his confidence in the thought that hope was not only sweeter than despair but infinitely more efficacious in encouraging the sustained efforts that the progress of liberty would require. And he also knew, with the certainty born of human compassion and fortified by close observation of human nature, that "the mass of mankind has not been born with saddles on their backs, nor a favored few booted and spurred, ready to ride them." This palpable truth Jefferson had known for some years before he wrote the immortal phrases of the Declaration of Independence and found it possible to reaffirm a full half-century later, in the spring of the year when he died.

CHAPTER IV

Hamilton and the Pursuit of Power

IN the pursuit of understanding Hamilton, it may be profitable to begin by considering the odd pattern of Hamilton's reputation in the century and a half since he died. In the 1790's, at the height of Federalist-Republican antagonism, Jefferson called him a "Colossus" to his party, "an host within himself." Yet approximately a half-century later, in the era of Jacksonian populism, when American political life was dominated by Jeffersonian democracy and the sentimental appeal to Jeffersonian ideals, Hamilton's reputation was at its extreme low ebb. Despite all obstacles, however, his family waged an aggressive and unrelenting fight to establish Hamilton as the greatest of the founding fathers, and after the Civil War the transformation of America into an industrial society provided the environment to support this long-cherished family ideal.

It is today, however, that Hamilton's prestige rises toward an ultimate summit. In domestic politics, the increased importance of the national government in both political and economic affairs increases the stature of Hamilton as the man who affords an invaluable historical precedent for policies that extend governmental power and regulation. In international relations, the rise, first of Nazi Germany and then of the Soviet

Union, to domination of the world scene has led many observers to regard Hamilton as the most far-sighted and seminal statesman in the American tradition, for the problems created by these aggressive modern totalitarian states have been an invitation to the kind of political "realism" in American foreign policy that Hamilton favored. But most of the recent and current tributes to Hamilton make him the prophet of American capitalism, the *real* maker of the American nation. We must remember that the 1940's and 50's have witnessed a new role for the large corporation, along with a conception of "dynamic" capitalism that replaces the earlier "stagnant" capitalism associated with the depression thirties. In political ideology this same period has seen the creation of a "new" conservatism, linking a reverence for tradition and property (under God) with the improvised and new forms of capitalistic growth and organization.

We found ourselves, at the time of the bicentennial celebrations, in a climate of thought surrounding Alexander Hamilton that carried us back to the high opinion of him once confided to Timothy Pickering by John Marshall—that he was certainly one of the greatest men that ever lived! It is possible that we have moved from the failure, a century ago, of not taking Hamilton seriously enough, to a present effort to take him forcibly beyond his human scope. The margin of uncertainty that has surrounded Hamilton brings to mind a sentence of William Butler Yeats, "A man walked, as it were, casting a shadow, and yet one could never say which was man and which was shadow, or how many the shadows that he cast." If we fail to understand Hamilton, to discriminate between the man and the shadow, we can neither understand the American political venture nor assess its glory and its shame.

What follows will not dissipate the many shadows Hamilton cast. It should help, however, to present some serious objections to the kind of encroaching shadow that distorts our present landscape of belief. Hamilton certainly achieved some work for which his contemporaries found him important and all future generations should find him influential. It was Hamilton who played the most active role in quickening the process that led from a financially impotent federation to a financially functioning central government. It was also Hamilton who seized upon the "broad" interpretation of the Constitution to stretch its vulnerable clauses as protection for the growth of federal power. In this sense, the work of Hamilton and the interpretations of Marshall are properly seen as a continuing logic as well as a shared interest. But above all, it was Hamilton who nourished the prophecy of an ever-expanding American industrial economy—a prophecy that he tried, too precipitately, to convert into immediate policy, but a prophecy, nonetheless, that can hardly be considered irrelevant to our present strength.

1

Hamilton's greatness, I believe, lies in the brilliance that gave him the vision and boldness to see the vast potentialities for economic development in the new country. To put it simply and perhaps crudely, but accurately, he advanced the theory of industrial capitalism in a national, American setting. He advanced this theory almost *ab initio,* moving free of the great influence on general thought of Adam Smith on laissez faire, of the physiocrats on the primacy of agriculture, and of the simple mercantilist philosophy which was under attack from both groups. Smith's influence on those who accepted the laissez-faire tradition was such as to blind them to both the necessities and the realities of economic power. They were led, ultimately, to a theory of pure competition, in which the state's primary function in economic matters was to protect private property rights as long as these remained small and in private competition with each other. But they ignored the constant development of real economic power, which was made necessary by the advance of large-scale investment in fixed capital, and which was responsible for the continuous increase in productivity. The fact of large-scale private investment is opposed to the theory of pure competition, but this fact is with us today, together with high standards of living and strong labor organizations. This is the fact of workable competition, which is associated with advances in technology and limits on economic power established by competition in substantial parts of the economy among a few large firms in important industries. Until our time we had not even felt the need for a theory of workable competition to account for the success of American capitalism as we know it.

Hamilton advanced three fundamental propositions that have a significant bearing on the issues of power and morals. First, he saw the possibilities for the development of private capital and the national gain resulting therefrom. Second, he advanced, almost without precedent in his time, a systematic government program for promoting the development of private capital. And third, he provided the basis for a political theory that associates democratic with industrial, capitalistic progress. Let us consider each major principle in turn.

First and most patent was his recognition of the great importance of private capital, both in finance and in manufacture. Here Hamilton was, basically, converting the doctrine of Adam Smith to a genuinely American perspective. But he was doing more, and in this was anticipating later developments. Smith was primarily concerned with the benefits to be derived from the division of labor—the prospects of profitable trade that could be achieved in a society of artisans where many workers were employed to perform individual segments of a total job. Ricardo's advance over Smith was the introduction of the idea of fixed capital associated with machinery. But Ricardo failed to appreciate fully the importance of money, which he treated as a veil. Hamilton was practically alone in his appreciation of monetary matters and of what he called simply the moneyed men. It is this recognition of the importance of investment in banks and factories with new machinery and the prospects of private property that is most consciously advanced by Hamilton. He was indeed alone in its theoretical, as distinct from its immediate practical, defense in the United States.

On these matters of central economic doctrine Hamilton stands in opposition to Jefferson. For Jefferson, alive to the new ideas in his day and to the conditions of the American economy as he knew and loved it, was attached to the physiocratic belief in the economic and related political and moral primacy of the independent farmer. He was also an advocate of those parts of the Smith doctrine that would deny the state a positive role in economic matters and would promote free trade and its related government policies. His intellectual support of these ideas was most active, as is seen in his constant interchange with the French economists, Turgot, Say, and Du Pont de Nemours. And finally, Jefferson saw in England, to a lesser extent in France, and most deeply in the changing face of his own country the harsh changes that the industrial revolution visited on the people in the cities and in the rural areas. He decried the hurried and malformed growth of cities, which denied a sense of community to the working population and therefore resulted in self-alienation —a loss of identity, integrity, and independence—and an ultimate loss of morality. But Hamilton had the greater, bolder, more realistic vision in these matters of economic development. It was this vision that made Hamilton write, in his masterful *Report on Manufacturers,* "Everything tending to establish substantial and permanent order in the affairs of a country, to increase the total mass of industry and opulence, is ultimately beneficial to every part of it. On the credit of this great truth, an acquiescence may safely be accorded from every quarter."

Hamilton's second great contribution was the proposition that it is necessary for the government to create the positive conditions for economic growth. This is the true significance of the constant conjunction of government and property in every one of his proposals. As early as 1779 he wrote, on the pressing issue of the deplorable state of the currency, as he had witnessed it in detail while assisting Washington to obtain funds for the Revolutionary effort: "The only plan that can preserve the currency is one that will make it the immediate interest of the moneyed men to co-operate with government in its support." He outlined in this letter practically all the measures that were ultimately put forward in his great reports to Congress and concluded it with a statement of complete confidence in its practicality, because, as he said, it "stands on the firm footing of public and private faith, . . . it links the interest of the state in an intimate connection with those of the rich individuals belonging to it, . . . it turns the wealth and influence of birth into a commercial channel, for the mutual benefit, which must afford advantages not to be estimated."

At the end of the same year there was another letter in which he dealt with the steps required to raise revenue and support the national credit. It was this letter that detailed a charter for a national bank incorporated under both private and public auspices. Here we have the core of his philosophy of the active role of government, which is the basis of his great theory of the implied powers in the Constitution. For the bank would, as Hamilton so clearly saw in this early period,

erect a mass of credit that will supply the defect of moneyed capital, and answer all the purposes of cash; a plan which will offer adventurers immediate advantages, analogous to those they receive by employing their money in trade, and eventually greater advantages; a plan which will give them the greatest security the nature of the case will admit for what they will lend; and which will not only advance their own interest and secure the independence of their country; but, in its progress, have the most beneficial influence upon its future commerce, and be a source of national wealth and strength.

And then he concludes with a principle that we have only come to appreciate in our day:

A national debt, if it is not excessive, will be to us a national blessing. It will be a powerful cement of our Union. It will also create a necessity for keeping up taxation to a degree, which, without being oppressive, will be a spur to industry.

All his great reports on the public credit, on the public bank, and on manufactures are further public elaborations of this boundless faith, which he had already crystallized in his private correspondence while still a young man in his early twenties.

Hamilton's third contribution went beyond the purely economic terms involved in the first two, to what is in essence a political theory: that a federal government, with positive safeguards for the people, is only possible where the government secures the rights of private property. Whereas Hamilton was willing to argue the other principles, he largely assumed this one. As a consequence, there is a natural criticism of this view which tends to consider it as basically opposed to democracy rather than a condition for it. Support is lent to this interpretation from two very different sources—the great influence of Jefferson and the more insidious but nonetheless powerful influence of Marx. Jefferson, as we saw, decried the effects of the industrial revolution but failed to foresee the importance of the expansion of capitalism in lightening man's burdens, freeing him for the cultivation of mind and spirit (which Jefferson valued so highly), and thereby strengthening democracy. Part of this failure, of course, was due to unregulated speculation and investment, which did create evils and which, uncontrolled, could have destroyed democratic society.

Marx, on the other hand, has influenced those who criticize the Hamiltonian program by claiming that the protection of private property is inconsistent with the common good and that only social ownership or control of the large-scale means of production will assure real—because, they allege, economic —democracy. I believe we have now learned something of the consequences of national ownership of the all-important means of production, and what we have learned is that where a government is directly responsible for the level and character of total employment and total production, there is a tendency for it to become a total government. For in order to assure the success of a total economic plan, the state tends to assume control of labor and ultimately of the political opposition, whether this is deemed necessary in the name of the people or of the state.

In this new setting Hamilton's advocacy of private property finds, I believe, a new defense, which permits us to see stronger democratic tendencies than are normally held to flow from private property. These fall into four areas: First, property that is private can never be as strong as the government, as long as the government will use its powers to protect itself. Second, the exercise of private property rights is not always harmonious; on the contrary, private interests very often compete with each other. Third, the competition of large aggregations of private property promotes strong combinations of other private groups, who want to check the power of others in order to protect their own economic position and advance their own political position in industrial society. And, finally, the resulting increase in productivity leads, in a democratic order, to increased leisure, which permits more and better education for the good life in Jefferson's own terms.

In assuming this principle, Hamilton too easily assumed the common good to flow from property and neglected to point out and correct the known evils which industrial democracy has now measurably overcome. What is more, he even praises some of these evils, as in the case of his proposal to place young children and women in the factories. Hamilton thus failed to frame his program in deliberate moral terms and sometimes even advanced immoral ends in order to promote property itself.

2

The bearing of these considerations on the question of power and morals should now be plain. Of the five men we are discussing, Hamilton had the sharpest vision of an infant nation's need to acquire national strength, both economic and military. In stressing this and providing a program for the deliberate encouragement of productive and capital strength in the United States, he was—as we now see—a reliable prophet of the mightiest industrial economy the world has yet produced. And there is no wisdom in belittling the contribution of a richly productive economy to the basic welfare of the people as a whole. This is certainly one of the foremost virtues of a democratic society, that it can offer most of its people freedom from the grinding misery of a subhuman struggle for bare life. The direction of Hamilton's thought to this constructive end was good fortune for this nation.

These achievements cannot be effectively denied by any critic—whether for partisan political reasons or any others. But what we must ask is where such achievements and the kind of talent Hamilton unquestionably had would have led us if they had been the preponderant elements in the American political tradition. For although we can, with Aristotle, properly regard economic goods as the indispensable means for the good life, they are surely not its self-sufficient end. A certain amount of external economic security is ancillary to leading the life of reason, spirit, and liberty. Hamilton's normal outlook is bounded by the production of these economic means. It is not bathed in the open light of larger human and spiritual ideals. Franklin, on the floor of the Constitutional Convention, expressed a conviction which opposed that expressed in Hamilton's single speech to the Convention and which accords completely with that of Jefferson, who could not express it himself because he was out of the country. Franklin disliked "everything that tended to debase the spirit of the common people" and warned that should the American Constitution betray great partiality to the rich, its influence in the world would be harmed, and this harm, inflicted because we had deserted moral ideals, would ultimately boomerang to injure our power. Franklin's concern here, like Jefferson's, for attracting common people to this country, was farsighted, as was Hamilton's concern for developing the nation's wealth.

In this context, we see two important issues for democracy in our time. The first involves the role of the expert. This presents a serious political problem in a complex industrial society that wants to maintain its democratic ethos. Hamilton was not only an expert in financial matters but really believed that only those who are expert, a quality he associated with the rich and the well-born, should control. To overcome the dangers implicit in control by experts, it is necessary to provide mechanisms for assuring that there is constant confrontation of experts so as to bring to light the different issues of fact and value implicit in all policy recommendations. This is most important, because there is a magical aura that surrounds the role of the expert, which is a danger to democracy.

The second issue involves the relation between economic means and human ends. Jefferson and Hamilton each emphasized one of these terms exclusively, rather than their dynamic balance. But in noting this failure we are in fact noting a failure that has not been made up even in our day. The problem of human ends and economic means, employing both sets of terms from Hamilton and Jefferson, remains an urgent unfinished task in establishing the philosophy of democracy for contemporary society.

Central to any meaningful interpretation of Hamilton are his views about power. This is the paramount object of his concern, both as thinker and doer. Since there is an intimate union of personal conduct and theoretical preference in Hamilton's pursuit of power, it will not do to confine investigation to only one of these two connected phases. It seems to me that two fundamental questions must accordingly be asked about his pre-emptive interest in power. The first is: How did he view the role of power in his political thought? The second is: What did he value power for, and specifically, in the linkage of thought and action, for whom did he want it?

3

A natural starting point for understanding Hamilton's view of power is his contribution to the *Federalist Papers*. In these papers he rejects utopian theories that promise "an exemption from the imperfections, the weaknesses, and the evils incident to society in every shape." He will concede nothing different to what some have called "the genius of republics." And given such a character for man, Hamilton sees all society in terms of power—either the love of power or the jealousy of power. Politics is the supreme power struggle. Thus, although Hamilton professes his attachment to republicanism in the *Federalist Papers,* his view of power causes him to emphasize a "strict and indissoluble Union," a "consolidated system," where the states should be "in perfect subordination to the general authority." In this context he could not go as far as he wished in depreciating the role of the states, but he adverted to the greater danger that the state governments would encroach on the Union, than that the federal head might encroach on its members. His great fear was that "they will finally sap the foundation of the Union."

There is little doubt where Hamilton "catches fire" in the *Federalist Papers*—it is where he glimpses the potential might of the American nation. "Let the thirteen states . . . concur in erecting one great American system," he exhorts, "superior to the control of all transatlantic force or influence, and able to dictate the terms of the connection between the old and the new world!" For such a system plenary powers are necessary for the government, since its policy must always be to "increase its garrisons against others; whereas to control the internal life of the nation from inevitable maladies like sedition and insurrection, these powers ought to exist without limitation."

Hamilton's conception of energetic power joined political power with money. "Money is, with propriety, considered as the vital principle of the body politic," he wrote. Only where the men who govern are the moneyed few can one rightly expect to have energetic government. The missing link in this argument he readily supplies; only moneyed men have "so great a personal interest in the government" that no means to bribe them can be resorted to. Apparently all other men, who have only life, liberty, and the pursuit of happiness at stake, lack an equally personal interest in government and are not safe from the temptations of bribery. Thus, Hamilton's militant, wealth-oiled nationalism drives toward unity in an almost monolithic sense.[1]

4

Since Hamilton's view of power in the *Federalist Papers* is tempered by a sense of practical urgency in securing ratification, one can gain a better appreciation of the extent of his mastering preoccupation with power by glancing at some of his arguments on other occasions. When real issues arose, how did Hamilton's views of power take on operational meaning? He showed himself willing to use coercion and force. Though there are several important instances to cite, one early occasion will suffice—the Newburgh Affair. When military victory was achieved in 1783, Congress was embarrassed by urgent demands made upon it by a group of public creditors and by a deputation of army representatives—the latter pleading for compensation for past services. Several nationalist politicians, including Hamilton, joined forces with certain army officers at Newburgh to try to secure national revenue and the kind of government they had so far been unable to achieve. Hamilton attempted to get the support of General Washington, to whom he wrote: "The great desideratum . . . is the establishment of general funds, which alone can do justice to the creditors of the United States. . . . In this influence of the army, properly directed, may co-operate." When Washington angrily

[1] For contrast, see the Madisonian view in the *Federalist Papers*, as interpreted in Chapter VI.

condemned the suggestion and flatly refused to use the army in this desperate political way, Hamilton wrote at length in an effort to conceal his own part in the plot, but in further correspondence he observed: "I cannot myself enter into the views of coercion which some gentlemen entertain, for I confess could force avail, I should almost wish to see it employed. I have an indifferent opinion of the honesty of this country, and ill-forebodings as to its future system."

Hamilton's views as expressed during the Constitutional Convention are also enlightening. There he showed clearly enough by the tenor of his proposals that the political system he preferred was not a republic (which he despaired of) but a constitutional monarchy patterned on that of Britain. The people are turbulent, unreasonable, activated by passions primarily; every man, he said in approval of what he thought David Hume had pointed out, is a knave. How could knaves be trusted to guard the national interest, to keep the nation strong and not deliver it in bondage to hungry powers from abroad? Create permanent barriers to pernicious innovations, he answered. Follow the pattern of the British government, which he judged "the best in the world." In the Constitutional Convention he confessed his grave doubts "whether anything short of it would do in America." Societies naturally divide into two basic political divisions—the few and the many. Each group has distinct interests. The few, the aristocracy, are the propertied men whom the British government draw into their House of Lords, "a most noble institution." These men, having nothing to hope for better than what they have, resist change, and thus act to stabilize the role of the Crown and the Commons. The king's interest, also, is so enmeshed with that of the nation, and his "personal emoluments are so great, that he is above the danger of corruption from abroad." Meanwhile, the Commons is held in check by both the monarch and the aristocrats, and Hamilton piously wrote into his notes for the Federal Convention that "there ought to be a principle in government capable of resisting the popular current."

Human nature, then, is to be controlled by vigorous execution of the laws. On this last point Hamilton's notes for his major address in the Federal Convention furnish a valuable gloss. He wrote: "It is said a republican government does not admit a vigorous execution. It is therefore bad; for the goodness of a government consists in a vigorous execution." That meant that the major motivations of human nature—the passions of avarice, ambition, and interest, which govern most individuals and public bodies—must be made to flow into the stream of the general government. With regard to any kind of state "sovereignty," therefore, Hamilton saw no arguments that would mitigate the unqualified evil it would do to national unity and efficiency. "The general power, whatever be its form, if it preserves itself, must swallow up the State powers, otherwise it will be swallowed up by them." On this ground Hamilton wanted to go beyond either the New Jersey or the Virginia plans and do away with the states altogether. But having voiced this thought, he at once protested that he had not meant to shock public opinion by proposing such a measure!

When Hamilton realized that his proposals ran counter to the predominant republican sentiment in the Convention and that his plan for sweeping national powers and authority evoked alarm, he left the Convention. He wrote letters to Washington which reported a remarkable coincidence he could not help observing between public opinion and his own sentiments. By design, he managed to reappear on the scene in time for signing the Constitution. Thereupon he also urged others to sign, arguing, as Madison reports him, that "no man's ideals were more remote from the plan than his [Hamilton's] were known to be; but is it possible to deliberate between anarchy and convulsion on one side, and the chance of good to be expected from the plan on the other?" Although he did not vest confidence in republican government, as he had acknowledged during the debates, he would address those who did "in order to prevail on them to tone their government as high as possible."

This done, he returned to New York, where he realized that the prospects for ratification were dark. Governor Clinton opened the opposition with a series of articles, signed "Cato," to which Hamilton immediately responded under the signature "Caesar." [2] Hamilton stated his defense of the Constitution in terms that expressed his utter contempt for the people.

For my part, I am not much attached to the majesty of the multitude, and therefore waive all pretentions (founded on such conduct), to their countenance. I consider them in general as very ill-qualified to judge for themselves what government will best suit their peculiar situations; nor is this to be wondered at. The science of government is not easily understood.

Fortunately, Hamilton soon realized that this method of defense would not secure ratification for the Constitution. Therefore he tried another tack and agreed with Jay and Madison to dash off the *Federalist Papers*, managing to submerge his contrary views in order to make the best of the real opportunities that were open for a stronger national government.

Hamilton's concept of power again emerges clearly from his attitude toward the Alien and Sedition Laws. Persistent efforts have been made by his biographers and other interpreters to absolve him of having supported these laws, and some go so far as to represent him as a defender of civil liber-

[2] Jacob Cooke has recently questioned the long-accepted belief that Hamilton was the author of the "Caesar" letters (*William and Mary Quarterly*, 3d ser., XVII, 1960, 78–85). I do not find his case conclusive or even persuasive, since each of his grounds is open to questions of fact and interpretation in the light of the larger context of Hamilton's writings and actions. Two points, among many others, may be mentioned briefly here. One is the congruence of "Caesar's" sentiments with the views which Hamilton expressed in the Constitutional Convention. The second concerns Hamilton's remark that "the greatest man that ever lived was Julius Caesar." On the whole, I believe a strong case can be made in support of P. L. Ford's initial attribution of the letters to Hamilton.

ties who, with Marshall, even opposed his own party. The basis for these portrayals has been one hastily written letter Hamilton dispatched to Oliver Wolcott, criticizing a first draft of the Sedition Law—a version the Senate itself recommitted two days before Hamilton wrote his letter. From this point on Hamilton registered no further complaints, nor did he advise any mitigating amendments for the new measure that was substituted. He entered no protest when President John Adams signed the bill. Most important of all, once the Alien and Sedition Laws were enacted, Hamilton became a leading advocate of their enforcement, lamented the fact that President Adams failed to execute the laws more vigorously, and advised the Speaker of the House that "if the President requires to be stimulated, those who can approach him ought to do it." It became clear in 1799 that Hamilton was eager to protect the reputations of all federal officers from political criticism by enacting an even more severe sedition act than that of 1798! Since he had been appointed, early in 1799, a major general in the provisional army raised against France, he had a personal interest in shielding the reputations of federal officers from Republican criticism. The obvious correlation between Hamilton's behavior in this vital issue and the theoretical views we have already formulated, which show his hostility to factions, hardly needs to be stressed. The opposition political party was an unmitigated evil in Hamilton's picture of energetic government and might be eliminated under the banner of crisis and national unity—if only the Executive, the Federalist leaders in Congress, and the Federalist courts would act with resolution and speed.

The hostility which Hamilton had nourished all his life and had given cautious voice to in the Constitutional Convention became caked in gloom and dire predictions as he contended against the political opposition of ardent Republicans during his Secretaryship of the Treasury and, in his later years, when he had engineered the downfall of his own Federalist Party. "It is yet to be determined by experience,"

he wrote while in the Cabinet, "whether Republican government be consistent with that stability and order in government which are essential to public strength and private security and happiness." Republicanism, he feared, might not
"justify itself by its fruits." And the day before Hamilton was
killed by Burr, he wrote to Theodore Sedgwick that the real
disease of American society was "the poison of democracy."

5

Since "energetic government," for Hamilton, involved his
own assumption of power in order to realize his policies, his view
of power cannot be appraised realistically without understanding his personal ambitions. Despite his marked abilities and
brilliant talents, there is an oppressive narrowness about his
interests, a single-minded preoccupation with himself—his own
power, ambitions, prestige, reputation, maneuvers, intrigues
—that makes a striking impression upon anyone who reads
his correspondence and papers after reading those of Jefferson, Madison, and John Adams. Madison and Jefferson are so
genuinely devoted to what they call without affectation "the
cause of liberty," they are so emancipated in pursuing the
larger interests of true humanists, that one must construct
their private ambitions and personal desires from between the
lines of objective comment and thought. John Adams, that
John Yankee, is often ill-humored, melodramatic, peevish, and
vain, but he is an electric personality, filtering all experience
through his strongly independent personality and turning his
penetrating intelligence to a vast range of scholarly and historical inquiries. But Hamilton—Hamilton is another being.

It is a challenge to try to grasp the specific nature of this
complex and ambitious man, which was very different from
that of Thomas Jefferson. The two, Hamilton and Jefferson,
contrast sharply with each other and represent the personal as
well as the political extremes in the continuum of republicanism that we are trying to appraise in the context of power and

morals. A curious meeting once took place between the two that helps us to establish this contrast. Jefferson reports that Hamilton, on a visit to his rooms, saw his collection of three portraits and asked Jefferson who they were. Jefferson named them—Bacon, Newton, and Locke—and revealed his feeling for them as the greatest men of all time. Hamilton paused and then remarked: "The greatest man that ever lived was Julius Caesar."

Here we have two very different visions of man and society. One is a vision of luminous reason for the pure delight it gives and the supplementary power it provides. The other is a vision of energetic power, with instruments of military, political, and economic force to protect, sustain, and advance such power. The devotion to the image of Caesar does much to explain Hamilton's character. I am prepared to say this, not on the basis of a single remark reported by a political enemy, but on the basis of a study of his life, his lifelong correspondence, and his published papers and reports—materials that inevitably reveal more than they are meant to. Hamilton in his conduct and thought is the embodiment of an ageless theme, the pervasive drive for power. Oddly enough, he stated this himself with astonishing clarity and decision when he was a twelve-year-old child clerk in a West Indian trading house:

To confess my weakness, Ned, my ambition is prevalent, so that I contemn the grovelling condition of a clerk or the like, to which my fortune, etc. condemns me, and would willingly risk my life, though not my character, to exalt my station. I am confident . . . that my youth eludes me from any hopes to immediate preferment; . . . but I mean to prepare the way for futurity. . . . I shall conclude saying, I wish there was a war.

Hamilton, while still a young Revolutionary officer, expressed his admiration for Caesar as the master of the Roman world who broke with all ideas of democratic rule, despite his previous championship of the people, and treated them as unfit to share in the government. This political position is evidenced by a study of the excerpts Hamilton made in his Army

Pay Book from the books he was reading at the time, so different from those in the Commonplace Book of Jefferson. He copied the following from the *First Philippic* of Demosthenes: "As a general marches at the head of his troops, so ought politicians, if I dare use the expression, to march at the head of affairs; insomuch that they ought not to wait the event, to know what measures to take; but the measures which they have taken, ought to produce the event."

This view of Hamilton's ambition for power furnishes the key to the strange relationship he maintained with Washington. As a favorite aide-de-camp to the General at Revolutionary headquarters, Hamilton put up with his dislike for an office that implied, as he said, "a kind of personal dependence." Despite Washington's affection for him, Hamilton longed for high rank in the army and the chance to command an action; he determined that if the occasion for a break should arise, he would "never consent to an accommodation." He did everything short of direct assault to make the General yield him this opportunity. He was blocked for reasons which he never put in proper perspective. An episode did occur, Washington reproved Hamilton, and the latter adamantly tendered his resignation. The letter describing this episode contains the statement that "for three years past I have felt no friendship for him and have professed none" and urges the recipient to consider how his conduct "must have operated on a man to whom all the world is offering incense."

From this ungenerous beginning developed the close political association of Hamilton and Washington with which the world is familiar. For as soon as the war was over, Hamilton took up his correspondence with Washington, advising him on how to turn independence into a firm Union. Hamilton's suggestions flowed easily from a fertile and quick mind, and hardly a letter exists in the substantial correspondence from Hamilton to Washington—from the spring of 1783 until almost the moment of Washington's death—that does not carry its freight of advice, strategy, pointed information, and specific direction—an endlessly advisory, managerial correspondence on his part, shorn of every grace, but full of practical suggestions. Washington plainly came to depend on this resourceful party leader and found in him both the most articulate polemicist of his administration and a far-sighted Secretary of the Treasury who was eager to play the role of prime minister. In George Washington, Hamilton found a symbol and the way to that futurity he was tirelessly preparing. Whether he ever made up for that want of affection he describes in his early letter is doubtful. Washington was for him the figure the American people loved and trusted in some deep union of heart and head. As a cool analyst of popular passion and a brilliant, if not profound, propagandist, Hamilton knew that policies which would normally strike stormy weather would be put a long way toward port if Washington sanctioned them. His power over Washington grew more solid with the years, and when the Federalists felt that Hamilton had Washington's ear more than any other Cabinet member did, they felt themselves to be on firm ground. But almost to the day of Washington's death, Hamilton was still using him as an instrument for his own purpose—his endless ambition for military command. Hamilton himself leads us to glimpse the truth here by the words he employed when he learned of Washington's death: "He was an *Aegis very essential to me.*"

6

In Washington's Cabinet, Hamilton had an opportunity to illustrate his conception of energetic government. In addition to his tremendous activity as Secretary of the Treasury, he moved at cross-purposes with Jefferson as Secretary of State, conducting himself on many occasions as though he were the Secretary of State. In 1791, for example, when Britain refused to honor the terms of our peace treaty, Hamilton dealt on a personal and confidential basis with the British Ambassador and vetoed all of Jefferson's efforts to secure full and complete adherence to the American treaty. Thus, when Jefferson was compelled to send a stiff note to Britain, the British Ambassador complained to Hamilton and reported the meeting to his government in these words: "After lamenting the intemperate violence of his colleague, Mr. Hamilton assured me that this letter was very far from meeting approbation, or from containing a faithful exposition of the sentiments of this Government." Again, in 1793, when the issue of neutrality arose, Hamilton continued to make the British Ambassador a confidant of the secret Cabinet deliberations and advised him of his own views, even though they were opposed to the official policy. Aware of our position of neutrality, Britain issued Orders in Council to forbid all trade with the French West Indies and seized hundreds of American ships that disobeyed these Orders. When Jefferson complained of these infringements of American rights, Hamilton again privately informed the British Ambassador that he agreed with the justice of Britain's measures and her view of international law and could not be responsible for his colleague's opinions in the matter. When a new and harsher Order in Council was issued by the British, the country was in an uproar, in which even the Federalists joined, and the Embargo Act was passed. At this point Hamilton, who by his secret dealings and contrary policies had supported the British at every turn, himself turned on the British Ambassador. This serious meddling and double-dealing alone was a sufficient basis for Jefferson's resignation as Secretary of State.

A dramatic incident proved that Washington's troubled second administration was still performing as Hamilton wished. The incident was the so-called Whiskey Rebellion in western Pennsylvania in the late summer and fall of 1794. Trouble had been brewing since the news of the Hamilton-sponsored excise taxes on whiskey had hit these western farmers, whose only portable product to eastern outlets was the liquid, not the grain from which it had been distilled. Liberty poles, mass meetings, and riots in the four western counties of Pennsyl-

vania, in western Virginia, and south as far as South Carolina
were the sum and substance of the rebellion. On an earlier
occasion when trouble had broken out in Pennsylvania over
the same cause, Hamilton had urged military intervention.
The Secretary of the Treasury took a particularly hostile view
of the popular uprising because he was the author of the financial system, part of which was being attacked. Hamilton was
quick to find that the rioters were "Jacobins," riotous demo-
crats in his thinking, typical of Jefferson's followers. He urged
Washington to issue a call for twelve thousand militia. For a
pseudonymous article in the newspapers Hamilton formulated
the issue as: "Shall there be government or no government?"
Temporarily assuming the office of Secretary of War, Hamilton rode at the head of the large militia force assembled to
squelch the riots. The riots had virtually subsided by the time
Hamilton set out, but despite the distressing absence of an
enemy—Hamilton's troops everywhere encountered commis-
sioners who proclaimed the restored peace—Hamilton pressed
on farther, panting for "rigor everywhere." The army, under
Hamilton's direction, made hundreds of arrests, and Hamilton
himself made Washington believe that the rebellion had been
systematic and political in origin, started by the democratic
societies of Jacobin clubs to overthrow the government. As a
national figure, Hamilton suffered in prestige from his role as
an inquisitional knight, a military leader on horseback warring
on a vanishing handful of outraged farmers.

7

The ambiguities that inhere in Hamilton's relationship with
Washington must be set alongside the hostility and malice
that he showed to the second Federalist President, John Adams.
We must remember that Hamilton's normal habit was to accept prudently what prevailing public opinion made him
believe would not easily be given up. John Adams had distinguished himself early in the cause of the American Revolu-

tion. Jefferson had been so impressed with Adams' role in the first and second Continental Congresses that he had called him the "Colossus of Independence" and others had altered this to the "Atlas." Hamilton, meanwhile, had played an important role in securing ratification for the Constitution by his share of the *Federalist Papers* and his work in the New York Convention. But when the first administration was being formed, Hamilton yielded to popular respect for Adams, as vice president under Washington, although after some hesitation. As the conflict between Federalists and Republicans became more of a daily cockfight, both Jefferson and Hamilton requested permission to resign—the former on several different occasions. But Washington kept them close. After Washington's retirement it was essential for the Federalists to retain power to prevent Jefferson from capturing it; so Hamilton supported Adams. As unofficial adviser to Washington and "King of the Feds" Hamilton had placed three of his friends in the Cabinet—Wolcott as Secretary of the Treasury, Pickering as Secretary of State, and McHenry as Secretary of War —and a strange phenomenon developed when Adams took the reins of government from Washington: a Cabinet loyal to and obeying the orders of one man but that man a private citizen. Hamilton was making a figurehead out of the President.

The feud that broke out between Hamilton and Adams was in every way worse than the cutthroat rivalry which existed between the Republican and the Federalist chiefs. Jefferson hated contentiousness and reflex hostility, but he was Hamilton's match and better than Hamilton in building himself loyal organizational support. John Adams had been and always would be an "independent"—quarrelsome, impetuous, learned, and lacking the urbane art that conceals art, which Jefferson possessed. He was no match for Hamilton in a political fight, because Hamilton would revert to every intrigue and subterfuge to undo an enemy.

A dramatic incident occurred early in the administration of Adams, when war with France seemed imminent. Hamilton wanted no war but a state of "mitigated hostility" to permit the creation of a standing army. He knew that Washington would be invited to command the army, but he also knew that Washington was old. Therefore he maneuvered to have his obedient agents in Adams' Cabinet propose him as second in command, which they promptly did. Blocked by Adams, Hamilton appealed to Washington to threaten his own withdrawal unless Hamilton was approved. Thus the work of creating the new standing army fell upon Hamilton. He saw it as a defense in a possible war against France, the devil's own country. He saw himself commanding it "to subdue a refractory and powerful State," Virginia, for its opposition to the Alien and Sedition Laws. And finally, he saw himself as the gallant man on horseback seizing from Spain all her vast dominions in the Americas. "Besides eventual security against invasion," he wrote, "we ought certainly to look to the possession of the Floridas and Louisiana, and we ought to squint at South America." In all this we have the vision of a Caesar thirsting for military glory and expanding his country's empire. But Adams' sudden resolution to negotiate with France to re-establish peaceful relations, and to effect this independently after dismissing the Cabinet members who had been Hamilton's men, put an end to Hamilton's military fantasy.

One may be startled to realize that Hamilton, who adored power in government, who desired the most "mounted," high-toned government the American people would put up with, who spoke of an authority that commanded order and created stability for society, was in his own nature totally unfitted to do anything but work as a lone intriguer, a manipulator of others for his own political designs. In contrast with the collaboration of Jefferson and Madison, we must put the vengeful, deceitful, deadly pattern of cross-purposes that Hamilton inflicted upon the other leading Federalist, John Adams. No event in American history is quite so baffling and so irresponsible as the appearance of Hamilton's document against Adams in the months prior to a national election. The pamphlet,

called *The Public Conduct and Character of John Adams,
Esq., President of the United States,* provided a spectacle of
the two most powerful Federalists in the country locked in
ugly and mortal conflict. Hamilton knew that when he used
his funded authority and leadership to vent his ungovernable
temper on Adams for pulling the rug from under his military
boots he was inflicting cruel punishment on Adams and thereby
destroying the Federalist Party and his own political leadership. Hamilton always maintained that he had not meant the
pamphlet to get to the public, that it was written for a few
party leaders only. But, as he might have expected, the pamphlet did get out and presented to the American public the
display of a mighty leader of the Federalist Party arguing
against the competence and suitability of the Federalist candi-
date. Could Jefferson, in his First Inaugural Address, have
dared to say, "We are all Republicans, all Federalists," without this Pyrrhic victory of Hamilton over Adams?

I have avoided mention of Hamilton's ferocious behavior
toward his old collaborator, Madison, and toward Jefferson,
partly because such ferocity is assumed by some to be a natural
concomitant of opposing party chiefs and partly because violent
enmity tends to create an infected response. One fact, however, must be taken into account in Hamilton's antagonism
toward the Secretary of State (Jefferson) when he was Secretary
of the Treasury. It was suggested many years ago by John
Quincy Adams that Hamilton's ambition was "transcendent,
. . . his disposition to intrigue irrepressible," that he was
"violent in his personal enmities, and little scrupulous of the
means which he used against those who stood in the way of
his ambition." Much of Hamilton's hostility to eminent political leaders now appears to have arisen from his own ambition to be President. Since he could not declare himself an
aspirant to the office in the prevailing political manners of the
early Republic, Hamilton knew he must work for but not
reveal his ambition. In one of several articles he wrote to dis-
credit Jefferson, Hamilton projected his own secret ambition

and unscrupulous hopes on his opponent. A partially crossed-out section of this manuscript reads:

Mr. Jefferson fears in Mr. Hamilton a formidable rival in the competition for the presidential chair at a future period. . . . After he [Jefferson] entered on the duties of his station, the President was afflicted with a malady which while it created dismay and alarm in the heart of every patriot only excited the ambitious ardor of the secretary to remove out of his way every dangerous opponent. That melancholy circumstance suggested to him the probability of an approaching vacancy in the presidential chair and that he would attract the public attention as the successor to it were the more popular Secretary of the Treasury out of the way.

It is not hard to imagine why this article was left unpublished by its author, and why, even in its unpublished state, he thought it best to cross out the passage quoted. The distortion of reality which Hamilton evidences by charging Jefferson with his own design may not have been deliberate, but one can hardly fail to see in it a recklessness in his pursuit of power.

Abigail Adams, much disturbed at Hamilton's tactics in his effort to get himself appointed commander in chief of the army in 1798 wrote: "That man would in my mind become a second Buonaparty [*sic!*] if he was possessed of equal power." In Hamilton's private vision of himself as a Caesar he saw himself directing an energetic government, commanding an army, and working to create a vast American empire; and to bring this dream nearer to fulfillment, in an environment of sentiment for popular sovereignty, he became a practicing Machiavellian. He studied closely and analytically the realities of popular sentiment, current value preferences, and power groupings in his determination to employ all means (all are justified) in order to preserve the most energetic state.

8

There seem to be three different levels in Hamilton's complex theory and practice of power. There is first his private vision, then his practical strategy of means, and finally his more or less deliberate theoretical rationale. These levels may suggestively be associated respectively with the moral climate of Caesar, Machiavelli, and Hobbes. On no level does Hamilton seem aware that power is a runaway tiger, difficult to dismount.

Thus as a "realist," "power politician," or Caesar, as one who preached strength, stability, order, authority, and efficiency up and down the land, Hamilton was truly and utterly a failure. Those who hail Hamilton as the greatest "realist" in the American political tradition and as a prophet for our own times forget this. He recognized his failure two years before his death, when he wrote this unique comment upon himself:

Mine is an odd destiny. Perhaps no man in the United States has sacrificed or done more for the present Constitution than myself; and contrary to all my anticipations of its fate, as you know from the very beginning I am still laboring to prop the frail and worthless fabric. Yet I have the murmurs of its friends no less than the curses of its foes for my reward. What can I do better than withdraw from the scene? Every day proves to me more and more, that this American world was not made for me.

Had Hamilton been more successful in his various maneuvers to be the successor to Washington both in his military and in his executive roles, we would have had a different history. And why did he fail, we ask ourselves? First, because his own person and character were not such as to win sympathetic response from the people. Second, because those who opposed him knew how to exercise power to abate his ambitions and protect what they considered to be the common good. Here we see that moral concerns, when reflected in the character and in the thought of a leader, have a durable power—a power that Hamilton did not have.

I suggest, then, that Hamilton's failure to acquire the power he so dearly loved was due to a basic defect of character, an all-consuming passion for power. This passion arose from the need to objectify a basic insecurity in life, associated with his deep and deeply repressed feeling of injustice and shame in being born out of wedlock, poor, and without durable fatherly affection. He had to find his way alone in the world by the use of his wits. He sought to acquire security, and thus self-esteem, by outward success in the highest commanding social positions, whether in the army, the Presidency, or finance. Here we see the neurotic processes of a brilliant and obviously complex man whose *idées fixes*—energetic government, military command, British monarchy, and the sacred rights of private property—were all objective correlatives or rationalizations of his basic personal insecurity. This establishes the unifying thread in his constant seeking out of moneyed men and military leaders for his friends, his desire for commanding military and executive positions, his plan to marry only a daughter of the rich with social power, his hatred of the people, and his willingness to resort to subterfuge to achieve his ends. And now we see that even his brilliant economic program is of a piece with his character—brilliant because it presented a vision of the prospects of American capitalism which was dormant until our day, and characteristic because it was associated so completely with the claims of power that it ignored the moral ends of man. His bitter opposition to Burr was, I suggest, the fury of one who sees his opposite number threatening his position. They had, so to speak, to come to mortal blows. This is the dramatic meaning of Hamilton's death on the "field of honor" long after he had lost power and the possibility of recovering it. It was as if fate had come to punish him for his grave defect of character and consequent crimes with an early and violent death.

9

It should now be clear why I see some contemporary evaluations of Hamilton as frequently far too generous. Hans Morgenthau, for instance, in taking Hamilton's formulation of the national interest as the touchstone for foreign policy, ignores Hamilton's historic role and his failure to take account realistically of the international situation in his own time. Hamilton tended to equate the national interest with his own prejudices, as, for example, in his belief in imminent and inescapable war with France in 1798 and his consequent explosion with Adams. Perhaps even more important as a limitation on Hamilton's understanding of the national interest was his constant serious meddling in foreign negotiations, first while Jefferson was Secretary of State, but persistently throughout the three terms of Federalist administration.

Again, when Leonard White in *The Federalists* portrays Hamilton as the administrative genius, the model governmental organization man, he ignores the role of others in securing procedures for peaceful compromise and clean administrative order without violating a democratic-republican context. Administration cannot be treated in isolation from the all-important political objectives of guarding the individual and his liberties and, as instrumental to these ends, protecting the independence and limited powers of state and local government. In his study White also underplays Hamilton's habit of moving into the territory for which others were responsible—in the Cabinet and in other executive as well as in legislative dealings. Whether this is administrative genius or the genius to defy administrative order seems to be worth questioning.

A third current interpretation of Hamilton moves us directly into the atmosphere of the official bicentennial celebration: I refer to Louis Hacker's *Alexander Hamilton in the American Tradition*. Here, in making Hamilton the founder of the American nation, Hacker shows himself to be a victim of

Hamilton's own paramount preoccupation with power. He thus tends to equate means with ends, the triumph of American capitalism with the triumph of the American political tradition. There certainly are relationships between the state and the economy, but the economic relationships must play, and have played, a subordinate role in the development of American freedom. Hacker's evaluation is vitiated by its failure to account for two important factors: the fact that much of Hamilton's program was not accepted in the form in which he presented it, and the substantial contribution made by others in the establishment of an American political tradition. It is of transcendent importance today, when we are trying to make others recognize that freedom is in danger, to see that freedom is not synonymous with capitalism.

As a final example of contemporary interpretations of Hamilton there is Broadus Mitchell's two-volume biography. Although only the first volume has so far appeared, it is amply clear that Mitchell is attempting to create what we may call "the integrative Hamilton"—the man whose motive force was not love of power or personal ambition but the "office of generous patriotism." Mitchell views the conflict between Hamilton and Jefferson and their respective political philosophies as essentially an internal question, namely, "the wisdom of control or the philosophy of let-alone." Not content with one false dichotomy, he contends that two courses only were open to the American nation: "central authority or state volition." Hamilton thus must stand, Mr. Mitchell argues, as the wise patron of government guidance, possessed of the skill for "employing organized direction," not as the spokesman of property against the people, but rather as the creator of stability and system for a young nation, as one using the community of the rich for a "noble purpose"—to restore national credit. Hamilton, in Mitchell's view, must be credited with a "philosophical and moral" basis for his policies. To value him solely for his technical administrative and economic contributions to a developmental American economy is to deprive him of his great stature.

In one sense I believe I have argued against Mitchell's interpretation throughout. I can only add that without something akin to Madison's constant counsel that we seek the "requisite power" (enough to master challenges but carefully pruned and guided to preserve liberty) and without something like Jefferson's constant counsel that we protect the principles of self-government and the rights of the individual from state absorption, there would have been little in a Hamiltonian tradition to withstand the appeals of totalitarian "efficiency." Surprisingly enough, there would also have been little to withstand the onslaught of the Marxian social critique, which was directed against a powerful state defined as nothing more than the police arm of the capitalist class.

These "Conclusions" are hypotheses and suggestions about Hamilton and his place in the American political tradition. One luxury American historians should not indulge in is the illusion that Hamilton's ideas and practice are of no concern to us today. Never was the role of the state and its military defense system a greater problem for freedom. A realistic study of Hamilton should prove to carry some cargo of instruction for our time, but the contemporary evaluations of Hamilton which appear to have ridden the bicentennial wave have tended to be more visionary than realistic.

CHAPTER V

Adams and the Taming of Power

SALTY John Adams, with his perverse "go-it-alone" personality, bitterly predicted that "mausoleums, statues, monuments will never be erected to me. . . . Panegyrical romances will never be written, nor flattering orations spoken to transmit me to posterity in brilliant colors." His prediction was substantially correct and poses a genuine problem in the mysterious dynamics of "great men" in history.

Adams' intense patriotism made him ask to be considered "John Yankee, " to distinguish himself in blunt symbol from "John Bull." For John Adams, the so-called monarchist in the debate over Thomas Paine's *Rights of Man,* was much more truly and steadily a defender of what he termed "the aristocratical republic." In dealing with Adams' beliefs, it is always something of a question how much to trust any given thing he says, since that salty, testy, peevish, perverse, and yet brilliant mind indulges its prevalent mood without caution, in constant rebellion against the accepted, the conventional, the standard way of viewing events and ideas. But on the basis of a careful probing of his writings, it seems to me that, although John Adams may be understood as a conservative republican, he is primarily an *independent* thinker and statesman.

Adams' political philosophy is expressed in many lengthy

books and collections of articles, no one of which, he complained, had he had the time to abridge and condense, or arrange and methodize. What might be described as the inner core of Adams' political philosophy, after some labor to discount his temperamental exaggerations, is the principle of a working democracy, based on the precedent of the New England meeting hall and the training green, with the related principle of self-support for local schools, churches, and cultural institutions. All these democratic institutions Jefferson frankly admired as the "virtues" of Massachusetts, which he declared he was eager to try to inculcate in Virginia. The "town-meeting democracy," which Adams, in a sense, inherited, had actually been infused with fresh blood by his early and outstanding contribution to the cause of independence, and later by the powerful support he gave to high civic and educational ideals in his draft of the unique Massachusetts constitution.

In the longer view of political science and the theory of the state, Adams saw a different pattern. The main task of republican government (of any government that would try to avoid the pitfalls of despotism) was to prevent excessive power from passing into the hands of any one group. Villainy and human corruption are interwoven in all human affairs, but they increase when the stakes are highest—and consequently they are most virulent in the management of a great state. Politics, Adams once commented, has always been and still is "the sport of passions and prejudices, of ambition, avarice, intrigue, faction, caprice and gallantry. . . . Jealousy, envy and revenge govern with as absolute a sway as ever." The only secret he knew to offset this was that "power must be opposed to power, force to force, strength to strength, interest to interest, as well as reason to reason, eloquence to eloquence, and passion to passion." We must, in short, provide checks and compel agreement, to keep men safe within the legal bounds permitted his kind of government.

Thus, the only hope of improving the bleak picture of man's failures and society's convulsions (which Adams thought all history amply documented) is to devise a form of government "So mixed, combined and balanced, as to restrain the passions of all orders of men." In such providential checks and controls on power-hungry men, Adams saw the only hope for the people and the public good.

What he himself said he had preached as political gospel was the danger of absolute power, which was nothing else than "tyranny, delirious tyranny." Less than two weeks after he had been inaugurated as President, John wrote to his sympathetic Abigail:

Jealousies and rivalries have been my theme, and checks and balances as their antidotes till I am ashamed to repeat the words; but they never stared me in the face in such horrid forms as at present. . . . At the next election England will set up Jay or Hamilton, and France, Jefferson, and all the corruption of Poland will be introduced; unless the American spirit should rise and say, we will have neither John Bull nor Louis Baboon.

Thus in Adams' view he alone could steer an independent course for America and save the dignity and pride of the American republic.

1

Adams respected the rule of law and natural reason and in his revolutionary days was a passionate advocate of human rights. When he heard James Otis argue with impassioned eloquence the legality of writs of assistance, John Adams experienced what was almost a religious conversion. He perceived for the first time the key to an understanding of British-American relations—the authority of the British Parliament over the American colonies was limited by the fundamental law of the English constitution and by judicial review. In his autobiography Adams recalled: "A contest appeared to me to be opened to which I could foresee no end, and which would render my life a burden, and property, industry and everything insecure." Under the stress of this emotion he resolved to "take the side which appeared to be just, to march intrepidly forward in the right path, to trust in Providence for the protection of truth and right, and to die with a good conscience and a decent grace, if that trial should become indispensable."

This spirit gave impetus to John Adams' leadership in the political struggle for independence. Some time after hearing Otis he wrote his first sustained essay on law, *A Dissertation on the Canon and Feudal Law,* in which he expounds the inflammatory thesis that Great Britain is responsible for "an entire subversion of the whole system of our fathers, by the introduction of the canon and feudal law into America." Recollection that the encroachments upon liberty in the reigns of James I and Charles I produced many of England's "consummate statesmen"—the Brookses, Hampdens, Vanes, Seldens, Miltons, Nedhams, Harringtons, Nevilles, Sidneys, Lockes—Adams dares to say that the Stamp Act and other suppressive measures will in time convert Americans into the new engineers of liberty.

Volunteering to do more than write theoretical essays, Adams prepared a draft of instructions protesting the Stamp Act. These Braintree Resolutions were passed and adopted by forty other towns, something of a political success for the rising young lawyer. Subsequently, despite his growing hostility toward Great Britain, Adams played a singular part following the Boston Massacre. When the British captain, Preston, and the soldiers apprehended with him relayed their request that he assume their defense, Adams, realizing fully the unpopularity he would incur, accepted the task, for he believed it his duty to provide adequate defense for those who were accused; he was unyielding in his belief that good government depends upon the impartial operation of just laws. Fearing that the trial might have disturbing effects upon Adams as a potential revolutionary leader, the shrewd Boston politician Sam Adams sponsored his election to the Massachusetts House of Representatives. As a member, Adams served during that year on every important committee of the General Court, including the Committee of Correspondence, and added the training of a practicing politician to his undisputed skill as a legal thinker. When General Gage arrived in Boston some time later to close the port and shut the courts of the rebellious city, Adams found himself without legal work and was thereby enabled to throw all his energies into the political battle.

In 1774 when he was in the First Continental Congress, Adams presented a kind of home-grown compromise between mercantilism and laissez faire, denying to Parliament any legislative power over the colonies but affirming colonial consent to acts tending toward a monopoly of commercial advantages for the mother country. But the Second Congress was a different matter altogether. Since the First Congress, Massachusetts had experienced Lexington and Concord. In May, Adams, sick with a fever, rode to Philadelphia amid the rising excitement of crowds gathered to cheer the Massachusetts delegates on their way. All the forces of his nature—his capacity for moral drama (and melodrama), his militant and independent spirit, his pride and persistence, his power of observation, intellectual vigor, and legal skill—were on the alert. No wonder that he and Sam Adams and the "Massachusetts men" in general were resented as being "ahead" of the Congress, too impatient of measures like John Dickinson's conciliatory petition to His Majesty, too radical.

Realistic co-operation between the influential Massachusetts and Virginia delegates developed. From the Continental Congresses emerged an early North-South relationship of unique character and historical importance. John Adams, for example, pushing eagerly for the creation of a continental army and for independence, was the member who rose to speak in favor of delegating command of the army to Washington. Then, working hand in hand with Jefferson to revise the articles of war in an attempt to whip the new army into shape, Adams noticed a unanimity of outlook with the Virginian that he could not find, for example, with the conservative Philadelphia Quakers.

There is little doubt that in these busiest months of his life Adams earned his title of the "Atlas of American Independence." It was he who carried the burden of the fight for the Declaration of Independence, for which neither the Congress nor the people as a whole were entirely ready. Adams played brilliantly the difficult role of standing up and reviewing the complex chain of arguments and reasons for "Independence—now!" which gave rise to his most famous and seemingly most eloquent speech.

2

The measure for independence carried, John Adams, who had surmounted his provincial proclivities in working for continental freedom, engaged in the uphill strategy of forming state constitutions and cementing the states by a union. He also served on more than ninety different committees, of which he was chairman of more than twenty-five. Adams had the foresight to realize that planlessness and inertia could undermine the new nation's resources and security. Early champion of a United States navy, Adams thoroughly enjoyed his work on the naval committee. In addition, as head of the war board, he had the occasion to fulfill some of his suppressed military longings, working indefatigably, exhorting leaders on strategy, getting in contact with politicians up and down the coast for supplies and money, and urging discipline for the army so that "all men may be made heroes!"

Perhaps the most constructive contribution Adams made, however, was in coaching members of the Congress on the mysteries of government and constitution forming. Asked by George Wythe to put on paper some of his opinions concerning the fundamentals of government, Adams replied with an extraordinary letter, which was printed at the request of Richard Henry Lee as *Thoughts on Government* and which achieved considerable circulation among the members of Congress. Adams' conception of government at this time is an eclectic compound of representative democracy (on the model of English republicans like Sidney, Harrington, Locke, and Milton) plus the utilitarian formula that the "government which will produce the greatest quantity of happiness is the best." Happiness is defined after the fashion of seventeenth-century English Neo-Epicureanism, so that happiness is compatible with the dignity of human nature and, as Adams puts it, "consists in virtue." Special features of Adams' plan of government are his endorsement of the motto that "where annual elections end, there slavery begins"—a formula he later modified—and his insistence upon the "indispensable" provision for the "education of youth, both in literature and morals."

Worn out with the mountainous labors of Congress, Adams asked leave in October, 1776, to return to his home, where he looked forward to resuming his family life and his law practice and conferring with his constituents on affairs in Massachusetts Bay. But hardly had he returned to private life when Congress commissioned him plenipotentiary to the king of France, to serve with Franklin and Arthur Lee. His first foreign mission was a diplomatic fiasco.

But back home in Massachusetts, John Adams lost no time in drafting a constitution for his new commonwealth, the only state constitution in the United States that has survived to this day. In the preamble Adams states: "The body politic is . . . a social compact, by which the whole people covenants with each citizen, and each citizen with the whole people, that all shall be governed by certain laws for the common good." This concept of government, with its overtones of New England Congregationalism, contains further a unique provision for the encouragement of knowledge, literature, and the sciences to "countenance and inculcate the principles of humanity and general benevolence . . . and all . . . generous sentiments among the people." Before this draft was submitted, Adams again set out for Europe as Minister Plenipotentiary to negotiate peace and commerce treaties with England.

3

A most important by-product of Adams' years in England was his three-volume work, *A Defence of the Constitutions of Government of the United States of America,* perhaps the most sustained inquiry into the comparative history and philosophy of republicanism ever written by an American. Mountainous, repetitious, and in the main an eclectic collection of citations from Roman, Dutch, and English historians and political theorists, it is impressive in its keen commentary and broad scope. In a sense, the theme of this work is the intoxication of power. His country was about to construct a federal constitution and was troubled by popular uprisings like Shays's Rebellion. France was on the eve of a revolutionary crisis. Contemplating these events, Adams was fearful that a stable government of laws might give way to the ungoverned passions of men. In America faction and strife might destroy the independence for which he and countless others had labored so long. To provide a framework of stability capable of reconciling differences without violating the moral rights of individuals under law was Adams' objective.

In the republican theories of the past Adams thought he saw the magic formula that would stave off the inevitable corruption attendant upon other kinds of government. Absolute power was, he believed, "tyranny, delirious tyranny, wherever it was placed." This is the key to Adams' profound distrust of what he regarded as the "simple" democracy of Turgot, who had championed the principle of "government in one centre, and that centre the nation." This slogan Adams professed to be "as mysterious as the Athanasian creed." With all power centered in one legislative body, Adams was convinced, unchecked ambition would intoxicate the legislators, encouraging that selfish strife which ceases only with the victory of one man or one clique.

Adams believed that only in a government of checks and balances could a people provide for the continuance of govern-

ment limited by fundamental, constitutional law and characterized by legislation framed in the light of the *public* (not private
or group) interest. The balance of power resulting from such
"mixed" government would guard the republic from degen-
erating into democratic or aristocratic excesses. By "democracy"
Adams invariably meant direct nonrepresentative rule—what
Plato and the classical theorists typified as rule by the mob.
Given a choice between these two undesirable forms, Adams
believed that history would cast the balance slightly in the
favor of aristocracy as having been responsible for a little less
bloodshed, oppression, and chaos. Even in the desirable, mixed-
republican type of government, however, Adams warned that
there could be varying degrees of liberty, depending upon the
degree of balance achieved. In the separate chambers of the
aristocratic Senate and the popular House, mediated by the
"governor" or chief executive, who should represent the interest of the whole nation, Adams saw the temporary cure for
license, party or factional spirit, and the fruit of these—armed
conflict within a nation, when "Caesar or Pompey must be
emperor, and entail an endless line of tyrants on the nation."

Contemplating the springs of human behavior, Adams main-
tains that it is "weakness, rather than wickedness, which renders
men unfit to be trusted with unlimited power." His position is
a compromise between a Puritanical emphasis on human cor-
ruptibility and greed and the optimistic benevolence of a
liberal Unitarian. Emulation and the desire to prove oneself
superior to others are the primary motivations of men. The
impulse to help others Adams acknowledges to exist with overwhelming force in the few great and good patriots of history,
but he points out that these are too rare to raise the moral
level of unheeding society.

To the natural inequality of man Adams adds the social
inequalities due to wealth and family tradition, to chance and
education. Not concerned with the "artificiality" of the aristocracy created by such multiple factors, he insists that the inescapable fact of aristocratic influence in every kind of society

be honestly faced. Nor does he feel that the existence of individuals with more prestige and power than their neighbors is necessarily destructive of social justice. Popular welfare can be preserved so long as the accumulation of wealth and power does not become excessive. Adams repeats the classical argument that a city divided into the overwhelmingly rich and the desperately poor is a city bound to be torn by civil war. His strictures on unearned fortunes fortify the impression that he has enlisted himself on the side of a prosperous republic, with a large landholding and commercial middle class. Later, in 1811, commenting on political developments in Europe, he wrote: "The great and general extension of commerce has introduced such inequalities of property that the class of middling people, that great and excellent portion of society upon whom so much of the liberty and prosperity of nations so greatly depends, is almost lost; and the two orders of rich and poor only remain." In this he saw the cause of regal dependence upon the aristocracy, reversing the historical dependence of kings upon the middle classes in their fight against the nobles and the rich. And, evincing the same interest in the fate of the common people that has come to be identified with liberal "democracy," Adams comments that "the immense revenues of the church, the crown, and all the great proprietors of land, the armies and navies must all be paid by the people, who groan and stagger under the weight."

Thus, even the term "republic" was no guarantee of virtue in government, Adams felt. It could "signify anything, everything, or nothing." If one had a republic where the "profits of the few" would devour the "property of the many," there would be no order, no liberty, no "democracy." Frankly confessing his admiration for the British constitution, he later explained that he never had considered a hereditary executive or senate necessary—although critics of his *Defence* had asserted the contrary. "The limited, equipoised monarchy of England," he explained, "I have always thought the only government which could preserve civil, political, or religious liberty . . . in any of the great populous, commercial, opulent, luxurious, and corrupted nations of Europe." Should the contrasts of wealth become accentuated here as they were in Europe, and monopolies operate in a systematic way against national interest and against the welfare of the people, something other than a "mixed elective government in three branches" might be required. But such a decision, Adams wisely saw, would rest with the legislators who would survive in that far-off society.

In effect, then, Adams believed that "the people" had the essential share in sovereignty and that they could exercise final control over the "purse strings" through their representatives in the House and through the consideration given their interests by a nonpartisan Chief Executive. The aristocrats, he believed, would have no more than the power "isolated" in one chamber, the Senate. Here they could debate the troubled issues of the day, bringing their wit, wisdom, and learning to the clarification of national issues. They could, in Harrington's simile, divide the cake; but only the House could dispose of it.

4

Adams recognized the conservative drift of his recommendations—particularly for an age that was, he thought, beguiled by the flattering assumption of human innocence instead of depravity, and human equality instead of natural and inevitable inequality. Adams' approach to the great question of equality is that of a virtuous cynic—he wants to report what he thinks he sees and knows about human nature and history to confront the "hypocrisy" of those who pretend that men are equal. Adams' defense of inequality is based upon the recognizable differences in intelligence, attractiveness, birth, breeding, and wealth among men. These differences are natural and inevitable, he asserts, and whether we pretend that men are equal in some sense or not, wherever some form of superiority, such as good name, eloquence, or active ambition, is capable of winning the following of additional votes, we no longer have a democracy and no longer have men who are "equals." In a marginal comment (one of hundreds, I should say) on Rousseau's *Essay on Inequality*, Adams disposes of the notion that at a given point in the state of nature, "all equality vanished," commenting: "What equality was there before? Was the child equal to the mother? and the mother to the father? Not in strength, swiftness, understanding or experience." So that inequality is natural and social, and consequently it is properly political too.

In a fevered outburst against a passage in Mary Wollstonecraft's *French Revolution*, Adams inserted a marginal note which I think completes the picture of his views on inequality. He wrote:

And does this foolish woman expect to get rid of an aristocracy? God Almighty has decreed in the creation of human nature an eternal aristocracy among men. The world is, always has been, and ever will be governed by it. All that policy and legislation can do is to check force by force. Arm a power above it and another below it; or if you will, one on its right hand, the other on its left; both able to say to it, when it grows mad, "Maniac! keep within your limits."

As for the French Revolution itself, he summed up his judgment of the theory provided for it by the French philosophers by charging that Helvetius and Rousseau preached to the French nation *"liberty,* till they made them the most mechanical slaves; *equality* till they destroyed all equity; *humanity* till they became weasels, and African panthers; and *fraternity* till they cut one another's throats like Roman gladiators."

5

John Adams, in truth, personifies the repressive, authoritarian conscience. The only order he can conceive of is order from above and from so elevated a power that people will not be able to question it. Early during his first term as vice president, John Adams published a series of papers known as *Discourses on Davila*. The genesis of these controversial essays (which are a continuation of his *Defence of the Constitutions*

. . . *of the United States*) lay in the contemporary French espousal of unchecked popular rule. They were interpreted by exponents of democracy, however, as an attempt to recommend hereditary aristocracy and monarchy for America. This Adams denied vehemently, later stating that he was more an enemy to corrupt democracy. Only when carried away by his speculations concerning the ability of his new nation to preserve a healthy republican balance did he allow himself to entertain the idea of preferring well-ordered and limited aristocracy to rampant democracy rushing headlong into tyranny. The furor occasioned by these papers was heightened when Thomas Jefferson, as Secretary of State, sponsored Paine's recently published *The Rights of Man.*

Self-constructed order, intelligent co-operation in the voluntary compromising of interests—these Adams does not understand nor trust. Yet it is fair to remember that he does not trust the rich any more than the common people, nor the learned any more than the ignorant—for after all, it was the French philosophers who supplied their vile doctrine of equality to the service of bloody revolution. But what appears to be equal treatment for the people and the aristocrats—one sequestered in a lower house, the other in an upper—is an idea that Jefferson punctures neatly in a few sentences in a letter to Adams:

I think that to give them [the supposed "aristocrats"] power in order to prevent them from doing mischief, is arming them for it, and increasing instead of remedying the evil. . . . Nor do I believe it necessary to protect the wealthy; because enough of these will find their way into every branch of the legislation, to protect themselves.

Adams did not think too seriously about monarchy, however, once the shock of the French Revolution had subsided. He alternated between sanguine hopes that the free republic of the United States would prosper and gloomy fears that the virtues and habits of the people had not become sound enough to promise the success of the experiment. Sometimes he assumed an air of cosmic puckishness about his own (and others') po-

litical principles. The relinquishment of political power had
been deeply painful to Adams but when he came round to the
full life of books and private citizenry, he found himself not
only able to enjoy but able to transcend the old conflicts—
always to his own advantage! So when Benjamin Rush tried
to reconcile the one-time friends, John Adams and Thomas
Jefferson, Adams, who yearned for the reconciliation, pretended
to review the political differences that had separated them. He
claimed they were all frivolous—that "Jefferson and Rush were
for liberty and straight hair. I thought curled hair was as republican as straight."

6

It is a curious fact that John Adams, whose belief in a strong
executive was nationally known, proved to be a relatively weak
President. In face of the opposition of Hamilton and his followers, Adams' administration was destined from the beginning
to be a perilous one. Adams himself made a precarious situation
catastrophic by his inexcusable decision not to change his
Cabinet members, most of whom were Hamiltonian partisans.
Adams was truly, as Jefferson had observed, a "bad calculator"
of the "motives of men." In fact, his behavior as President is
almost as enigmatic as is his complex personality. On the one
hand, he was suspicious to the point of alienating those who
might have furthered his interests. On the other, where a more
judicious man would have sensed outright hostility and acted
accordingly, Adams possessed a childlike optimism. Thus,
weak where he should have been strong and strong where he
should have been weak, he pursued a course that led to his
own repudiation and accelerated the destruction of his party.

It was Adams' fate to be a leader without powerful followers.
Not enough of an Anglophile to please the Hamiltonian Fed-
eralists nor enough of a Francophile to win the support of the
Jeffersonians, he began his Presidency at a time when his

country hovered on the brink of war with France or with England or both. Out of this situation developed the great policy of his administration, a policy that Adams arrived at virtually alone and in face of sabotage of his Hamiltonian Cabinet and the most powerful Federalist leaders. Adams dedicated his administration to peace. And peace he achieved, even in the face of the overbearing actions of France, epitomized in the XYZ Affair, which precipitated, in 1798, an undeclared war with France. Added to this were the machinations of the Hamiltonian warhawks, who saw in the "war" the opportunity to form a lasting alliance with England and to establish a powerful standing army to throttle internal rebellion and extend American dominion in South America. Acting with unparalleled vigor, Adams cut the Gordian knot and appointed his own commission, which had the satisfaction of signing the Convention of 1800 effecting an honorable peace with Napoleon and France. This he rightly considered the outstanding achievement of his career and said: "I desire no other inscription over my gravestone than: 'Here lies John Adams, who took upon himself the responsibility of the peace with France in the year of 1800.'"

Adams' pride here is understandable. By that act he had cut himself adrift from the Hamiltonian warhawks in the Federalist Party. Privately, Adams had been aghast at Hamilton's headlong drive toward war—at his failure to ponder the suicidal implications of war with a mighty European power on the part of a struggling nation that was militarily weak (despite Hamilton's program). Adams made the decision, secretly and swiftly, to choose his own commission before the Hamiltonians could block him in Congress. When this commission signed the Convention of 1800, Adams felt indeed like a lonely "Patriot King." The Hamiltonians had panted for the war with France, seeing in it the opportunity to form a lasting alliance with England. When Adams made his magnificent decision to secure peace, he flung himself directly in the path of a whirlwind.

Hamilton, as we have seen, cut him down without mercy in the subsequent months, apparently thinking the ruin of his party not too high a price to pay for personal revenge.

7

The recovery of spirit that Adams effected in the twenty-six-year period of his retirement is as relevant to his character and contribution to the American scene as are the specifically political acts of his career. There is something breath-taking about his moral and intellectual energy as he converts himself from statesman to private philosopher. Never was Adams' writing so colorful, his reading so omnivorous, his friendships so brilliant and tender.

At first he had found his enforced idleness oppressive. He was appalled to realize that his fighting days were over: "when such long-continued and violent exercise . . . such frequent agitations of the body, are succeeded by stillness, it may shake an old frame. Rapid motion ought not to be succeeded by sudden rest." But it was foreign to his nature to remain long at rest. Almost at once he began a reply to Hamilton's attack on his Presidential policy. Tiring of this, he commenced his autobiography, but lost interest in it in his growing preoccupation with the battles raging in Congress. Disapproving as keenly as did John Quincy of Britain's impressment of American seamen, he increasingly supported Republican policy. By 1807 the man who had been branded as a monarchical Federalist sided with his son and the Jeffersonians in protesting the British outrage in the *Chesapeake* affair and endorsing the embargo. In the heat of the controversy following Jefferson's protective measure John Adams engaged in a series of bitter newspaper debates reminiscent of the days when he had occupied the spotlight of violent political drama. Always militant, he approved of the War of 1812 but could not refrain from criticizing its conduct and from writing impassioned letters concerning its prosecution.

There was always something of the armchair general about

John Adams. Throughout his life he had nourished a thwarted ambition to be a man of action, a soldier, a doer rather than a thinker. Always realistic, however, he ruefully speculated: "It is a problem in my mind, to this day, whether I should have been a coward or a hero."

Until his death he manifested a keen interest in international affairs. But he found more congenial reviewing the role he and his associates had played in the founding of the new nation, and like an old philosopher he pondered the laws of history, the nature of man, and the meaning of religion.

His political faith had become more firm and more liberal with his removal from the heated intrigues of political office. In certain important issues he was indistinguishable from the Jeffersonians—for example, his support of the Embargo policy and his approval of the Louisiana Purchase. He knew well the extremist plans of embittered New England Federalists to divide the Union, remarking that he had heard such plans on and off for about thirty-five years but that they had had no effect but to increase the attachment of the people to the Union. "However lightly we may think of the voice of the people sometimes," he confessed, "they not unfrequently see farther than you or I, in many great fundamental questions." He could now say with the authority of his years and his distance from power: "The Union appears to me to be the rock of our salvation, and every reasonable measure for its preservation is expedient."

8

John Adams' renewed friendship with Thomas Jefferson, after 1812, evoked an animated correspondence unparalleled in American history. Returning to his great theme of natural aristocracy, Adams reveled in the intellectual liberation afforded by a mind inquisitive and erudite as his own. When Adams and Jefferson tired of the pageant of changing civilizations, they mused on the subject of the religion of all ages and nations. It is interesting that two men so different in temperament, upbringing, and outlook should have arrived at such strikingly similar conclusions. For Adams ends by endorsing Jefferson's liberal and enlightened views, agreeing that the Sermon on the Mount is the key to true Christian teaching. Placing himself in the tradition know as Unitarianism, Adams confided that his prodigious study of religious literature had "made no change in my moral or religious creed, which has, for fifty or sixty years, been contained in four short words, 'Be just and good.' " Like Jefferson, Adams' contemplation confirmed his earlier liberalism: "My conclusion, . . ." he observed, "is universal toleration."

Professing an impatience with metaphysical reasoning somewhat belied by his own ratiocinations, Adams maintained that a study of ecclesiastical history tended to support agnosticism rather than positive theology. He therefore objected to the theology of even a renowned liberal like their friend Joseph Priestley, commenting:

You and I have as much authority to settle these disputes as Swift, Priestley, Dupuis, or the Pope; and if you will agree with me, we will issue our bull, and enjoin it upon all these gentlemen to be silent till they can tell us what matter is, and what spirit is, and in the meantime to observe the commandments, and the sermon on the mount.

The only concession Adams made to his agnosticism was the hope of a future life. Conventionally enough, his faith yearned for what his reason rejected and found strength in the fact that neither by revelation nor demonstration had the existence of life after death been disproved.

Indeed, the lifetime devoted to creating a new country became symbolic of the religious text Adams formulated in the clear perspective of his old age. Realizing that his faith in "reason, equity and love" must perpetually face the setback of human passions, stupidity, and selfishness, Adams stated that "after mature deliberation, I knew not whether I ought to laugh or to weep." He never permitted himself, however, the luxury of misanthropism. *"Homo sum.* I must hate myself before I can hate my fellow-men, and that I cannot and will not do." In the major moral crises of his career he had always wished to be governed by compassion rather than by jealous self-interest. This, more than any other characteristic, is the clue to his rejection of Puritan theology with its magnification of man's depravity.

John Adams had helped to make America vigorous, healthy, secure in its national boundaries, and devoted to equitable ideals. It troubled him in his old age that the delicate balance of the Republic might suffer as much from the encroachments of "stock-jobbers," the banks, and monopolies as it might from the multitude. Referring to "pure" or direct democracy (Adams believed that when "democracy" became representative, rather than direct, it was no longer democracy but republicanism), he wrote:

There never was a democracy yet that did not commit suicide. It is in vain to say that democracy is less vain, less proud, less selfish, less ambitious, or less avaricious than aristocracy or monarchy. It is not true, in fact, and nowhere appears in history. Those passions are the same in all men, under all forms of simple government, and when unchecked produce the same effects of avarice, violence, and cruelty.

In the long view Adams was prepared to admit that the eighteenth century had made progress in knowledge and self-government. In the past, revolutionists such as Sam Adams, Thomas Jefferson, James Otis, and himself had, by unremitting energy, altered the course of events. In a truer sense, however, the first immigrants to this country, the religious dissenters, were the "inventors and authors" of American independence. Thus Adams saw that the war on tyranny is, in its many stages, a perpetual one. He felt that the spirit of those who first protested against orthodoxy would have to be reborn before the science of government could advance. Only then, after trials, might greater freedom and juster laws be devised for all, for common people, for natural aristocrats, for the nation as a whole: "It is the decree of Providence, as I believe, that this nation must be purified in the furnace of affliction."

For a man who jested that he lacked the stoical apathies, John Adams withstood remarkably well the multiple misfortunes of extreme old age. In 1818 his wife, Abigail, died. His "Portia," his "dearest friend" through triumph and defeat, had been for over half a century his wisest counselor; with her ready sympathy and unfailing courage she had rescued him from the despondent moods that often assailed him. He never completely recovered from his loss. To his sorrow were added the natural afflictions of a man approaching ninety. He grumbled that he was not only old and sick but paralytic and almost blind. But, despite his feeble condition, he never lost the zest for living. Six years before he died, he attended the Massachusetts state constitutional convention and made his last public plea for religious toleration. Unable to hold a pen, he continued to dictate incredibly vivacious and penetrating letters. And when John Quincy was elected President, the old man experienced what was probably the most unqualified triumph of his career.

Five days before his death John Adams was asked to send a message as a toast to the July Fourth celebration commemorating the fiftieth anniversary of independence. He said: "I give you, 'Independence Forever!'" To Adams independence was more than an act of separation, more than a revolution. It presaged the ongoing history of a free and stable society. It was the fastness of law and a carefully devised Constitution. It was the recognition of a national character. It was the provision for tolerance and toleration. It was militant self-protection. Crowded into the phrase "Independence Forever," there were intimate values fully appreciable only by John Adams. When he was asked to add "something more" to it, he was imperious: "Not a word." He had said enough.

9

Thus John Adams managed to make his peace with the eighteenth century. In a letter to Jefferson he concluded that "notwithstanding all its errors and vices, [it] has been of all that are past, the most honorable to human nature. Knowledge and virtue were increased and diffused; arts, sciences, useful to men, ameliorating their condition, were improved more than in any former equal period." But he was troubled about the political developments of the nineteenth century: Would the new century extinguish all the lights of its predecessor? As though to reward him, the Adams family won itself a unique place in American life in that century. Some of the critics select the father's distinguished son, John Quincy Adams, as the greatest Adams; others, who consider the art of writing as superior to politics, accord Henry Adams first place. My own belief is that no later Adams can compete with the moral majesty and patriotic trust of the man who earnestly scanned his features in a mirror and pronounced himself in every way a "mediocrity." His hope for America's power and independence included his prayers for her maturity as a culture. With a touch of prophecy John Adams measured his young country "as yet simple and not far advanced in luxury," and declared:

The science of government is my duty to study, more than all other sciences. . . . I must study politics and war, that my sons may have liberty to study mathematics and philosophy, geography, natural history and naval architecture, navigation, commerce, and agriculture, in order to give their children a right to study painting, poetry, music, architecture, statuary, tapestry, and porcelain.

Some of these words have a homely, provincial sound. But the vision of progressive human needs is eloquent. This statesman's universe was large. John Adams did not exclude education, culture, and peaceful art, nor did he, like Hamilton, make a fetish of the pursuit of power.

As we review the careers of Adams and Hamilton, a curious

and ironic fact about them should give us pause. Their political enemies, Jefferson and Madison, who created the ideology of the Republican Party, were joined in a remarkable collaboration that they sustained for approximately a half-century without once striking a hard core of difference to diminish mutual regard and affection. On the other hand, Hamilton and Adams, who created the ideology of the Federalist Party, were participants in a remarkable pattern of cross-purposes, active distrust, and eventual hatred that was sustained by Adams until his final day in this earthly republic. As Jefferson came to recognize that his life was nearing a close, he wrote to Madison reviewing their joint work in the cause of liberty and enjoining his friend, "Take care of me when dead." Adams, however, confessed that his fears for the perpetual duration of our vast American empire and free institutions were heavy when he was "Cassandra enough to dream that another Hamilton, another Burr, might rend this mighty fabric in twain. . . ." The Republicans, in short, had not held the high view of power that the Federalists had—and yet they, not Hamilton and not Adams, had found the way to maintain and increase their power within the moral framework in which they placed their faith. At the end Adams could join Jefferson in opposition to Hamilton as the embodiment of power for power's sake and affirm his devotion to the American experiment for its dedication to liberty. They were also joined in their death on the same day— the day itself lustrous, for it was July 4, 1826, exactly fifty years after Jefferson wrote the Declaration of Independence, which John Adams had championed so valiantly that he won for himself the title of the "Atlas of Independence."

CHAPTER VI

Madison and the Workshop
of Liberty

AMERICA demands bold lines and strong personalities in
its public men. It might almost be said that unless a
man lends himself to caricature he will not be included in the
company of American political greats. James Madison has accordingly suffered unduly at the hands of American historians,
and he has suffered even more in being denied an appropriate
place in the affections of the American people. For my own part,
I should like to confess that I took for granted the prevailing
attitude about Madison, as in every way the junior lieutenant
to Jefferson, when I first began my studies of the American
philosopher-statesman. It was with genuine surprise that I
gradually came to realize that this gentle and modest man was
not the pure scholar who had wandered into politics, there to
be given favors of office by the great Republican leader with
whom he was closely associated. He was, as I have attempted to
demonstrate previously, in every way a full collaborator with
Jefferson in forming the Republican Party and in developing
that Republican ideology which is still unmatched in the modern theory of democracy. He was also the amalgamator of all
the essential elements in the Republican tradition, conceived
in the broad sense; for he achieved, in his thought and character, a total balance among Jefferson's ideals for the pursuit

of happiness, Hamilton's understanding of strategic means, and Adams' realization of the need to check power with power.

In this unique capacity as amalgamator, not only must we acknowledge Madison's contribution in designing the Constitution but we should at last be ready to appreciate the other important aspects of his political genius. Among these are his leadership in the first Congress under the Constitution; his advisory role to President Washington; his great share in the intellectual creation of the political ideals and beliefs of the Republican Party; his major contribution to the organization of that party; his strength as a diplomatist; and his firm and lifelong defense of the vital principles of government by majority rule with minority rights. It is also noteworthy that this even-tempered statesman was so absorbed by the great objects to which he gave himself that he almost never claimed anything for himself as a person, save that he hoped he had been able to make use of the opportunities offered him to advance the happiness of his country "and the hope of the world."

Madison's principles are of unusual interest today for a number of reasons. But one reason is central to all the others— the development and defense of the philosophy of democracy in strategic terms in a world where it is gravely threatened. Madison was an extraordinary scholar who looked to the past for what he could learn about democratic procedures, and who thus prepared himself to become the most informed member of the Constitutional Convention. He looked to the future, to the establishment of a free government which would have enduring power and yet enough flexibility to permit adjustments to new problems in a changing world. Finally, Madison was aware, not only of the value of establishing a long-range policy for the American republic, but also of the significance of the democratic experiment for the future of mankind. He nourished the deep hope that the American experiment would succeed and, in time, become a model for all people. It is in this ultimate bearing of his work and wish that he arrests the attention of the contemporary world; for he disposes us to ask whether our government can provide leadership which other nations can support and follow to maintain a free world against a powerful and aggressive political tyranny.

Madison's pointed message on America's role in the world is contained in an unusual letter which he composed at the close of his life, while in philosophic retirement. He wrote:

The free system of government we have established is so congenial with reason, with common sense, and with a universal feeling, that it must produce approbation and a desire of imitation, as avenues may be found for truth to the knowledge of nations. Our Country, if it does justice to itself, will be the workshop of liberty to the Civilized World, and do more than any other for the uncivilized.

In this revelatory phrase, "workshop of liberty," Madison caught the dynamic meaning of the idea of America.[1] There is an integral connection between Madison's thought of a workshop of liberty and Jefferson's ideal of the pursuit of happiness: first, because the pursuit of happiness involves the work and discipline of free men and, second, because the workshop of liberty makes the pursuit of happiness possible; it is a precondition of the happiness that is virtue. Here also we have a recognition of the strategic economic means that protect and advance liberty. Madison saw that the "great and advancing cause of a representative government" must marshal on its side continued prosperity in order to give the people relief from disintegrating sources of poverty and unemployment and in order to make good in fact its promised liberty and happiness.

If we go somewhat deeper into Madison's political philosophy, we will find at its core the function he assigns to power in relation to liberty. Madison constantly defends a political program or policy by showing how it protects, assures, or promotes the cause of liberty. On the other hand, he tries just as earnestly to secure liberty by assuring the appropriate powers necessary for its realization. His work is quite distinctive in its explicit and habitual counterpoising of these two elements, these two conditions for successful free government. Placed in

[1] For a more extended analysis of this phrase, see Chapter VII.

this context, one sees the significance of Madison's early efforts to assure a strong central government as a successor to the weak Confederation, but a government to be based on the sovereignty of the people and with its power limited by various checks and balances.

1

Madison's genius in compromising the opposed claims of power and liberty in the Constitutional Convention hardly requires review. For this role he has been hailed as the "father" of the Constitution. This is reflected in Madison's contribution to the *Federalist Papers*. It is generally recognized that Hamilton and Madison were able to join in this taxing writing enterprise because they had much in common. The two men had played a great role in the continentalist movement behind the Constitution, and the *Federalist Papers* was their joint effort to provide the political rationale that would wrest from the states the all-important ratification. But what is even now but imperfectly realized is that their views were far from identical—that one can, in fact, discriminate two different philosophies of power, the Hamiltonian and the Madisonian. Certain basic assumptions about human nature as relevant to the problem of government are, of course, common to both authors. They agree on what is ordinarily described as a "realistic" interpretation of human nature, that men are selfish, more prone to be governed by passion than reason, contentious, capricious, avaricious, and wicked; but they are less united in the degree of emphasis placed upon these qualities. Hamilton, for example, tends to exaggerate the tone of pessimism. He speaks of "the ordinary depravity of human nature," of the fiery and destructive passions of war that reign in the human breast, of "uncontrollable impulses of rage, . . . jealousy, . . . and other irregular and violent propensities." This leads Hamilton to stress a strong central government.[2]

[2] For further analysis of the Hamiltonian view, see Chapter IV.

For Madison, on the other hand, the glory of the federative system in the Constitution was its division of power between two distinct governments "and then the portion allotted to each subdivided among distinct and separate departments." He valued this distribution of power because it provided "a double security . . . to the rights of the people. The different governments will control each other, at the same time that each will be controlled by itself."

The outcome of these differences between Hamilton and Madison can be seen in their view on factions. One of the most interesting sentences in Hamilton's writings is his remark in the debate in the New York Convention that "we are attempting by this constitution to abolish factions and to unite all parties for the general welfare." This is not an isolated or unguarded statement but an expression of a consistent belief that the new union, if properly strong, could avoid the troublesomeness of the party system. No view could contrast more markedly with the universe of Madison's tenth *Federalist* article where the existence of factions is taken as the fundamental structural fact of a pluralistic, free society. Not that Madison supposes factions free of danger to society; but, as he says, we cannot cure a disease by killing the patient—cannot, that is, if we care about the patient. Factions for Madison were special-interest groups arising out of the fundamental conflict present in every society between those who are rich and want to maintain their riches and those who are poor and struggle to relieve their condition. "All civilized societies are divided into different interests and factions," he wrote in the interesting year of 1787, "as they happen to be creditors or debtors—rich or poor—husbandmen, merchants or manufacturers—members of different religious sects—followers of different political leaders—inhabitants of different districts—owners of different kinds of property, etc."

For Madison the great virtue of a republic is to provide that liberty which permits factions to breathe and to provide those internal and external limits on destructive license which encourage reasonable compromise of the multiple conflicting interests. He recognizes diversity, welcomes it, and provides for the kind of order that emerges from compromise and reciprocal controls. He is much concerned on all important questions with what he prudently calls "requisite power" and energy in government, but he invariably joins these necessary means with their proper ends—liberty, justice, and the rights of the people. Madison accordingly considers a republic "the least imperfect" of human governments; he has faith that it "promises the cure for which we are asking." Such wise tenets play no part in Hamilton's view of factions; the disease must be cured—let the patient beware. Thus, Hamilton's endorsement of the Constitution imperfectly conceals his disbelief: "I am persuaded that it is the best which our political situation, habits and opinions will admit."

The following passage in Number 10 of the *Federalist Papers* reveals the key to Madison's fundamental political thought:

As long as the reason of man continues fallible, and he is at liberty to exercise it, different opinions will be formed. As long as the connection subsists between his reason and his self-love, his opinions and his passions will have a reciprocal influence on each other; and the former will be objects to which the latter will attach themselves. The diversity in the faculties of men, from which the rights of property originate, is not less an insuperable obstacle to a uniformity of interests. The protection of these faculties is the first object of government. From the protection of different and unequal faculties of acquiring property, the possession of different degrees and kinds of property immediately results; and from the influence of these on the sentiments and views of the respective proprietors, ensues a division of the society into different interests and parties.

Madison developed a most important implication of his theory of factions for the support of a federal form of government. Where Hamilton wanted unity and felt that this could only be achieved by a strong central executive, Madison saw the feasibility and desirability of maintaining diversity within the United States. He saw this as being made possible by extending the operational sphere of real factions and by providing for their representation in a federal form of government still responsive to the people. On this ground he was able to reject the prevailing idea of Montesquieu that a republic required a small extent of territory. He went further and argued that, with a wide enough extension of territory, a more effective and durable republic could be established. For in such an extensive republic, with a multiplication of different factions and their appropriate representation, there could be secure interests and safeguards for both the exercise of majority rule and the protection of minority rights. On these theoretical grounds Madison was able to advance the need for a tighter federal union without requiring either the tyranny of the few or the tyranny of the majority to make it work.

2

One is also moved to admire the skill with which Madison developed his great theme in a series of papers he wrote for the *National Gazette* in 1792, defining the principles to which the Republican Party pledged adherence—papers that I have long considered worthy of separate publication and wide distribution for readers today. One essay on "Consolidation" described the natural tendency of government to follow a self-directed course when "the public mind" had no voice or was apathetic. The only way to counter such consolidation was to have an alert citizenry, whose close participation in local and state governments would permit them to express "the sense of the people" on important issues. Madison thought that the various authorities established by our unique federal system could be used to create "one paramount Empire of reason, benevolence, and brotherly affection." Another paper on "Public Opinion" declared it to be the agency to set bounds on every free government. Although Madison had not at first been in favor of the Bill of Rights, he had come to see the importance of Jefferson's arguments in its behalf; he had moved their adoption in the first Congress under the Constitution, and he now asserted that declarations of principles and rights had the important function of influencing public opinion and thus in turn creating further pressure in the direction of free government.

In a succeeding paper called "Liberty and Power," Madison pointed out that in Europe charters of liberty had, in some cases, been granted by established power, whereas America had introduced a new practice—to issue "charters of power granted by liberty." He proposed a formula for true republicans: "Liberty against power, and power against licentiousness." In a paper devoted to "Property," Madison distinguished between two major senses of the term: the first was the narrow sense, including money, possessions, and the right to exclude others from the objects we own; the second, the broad sense, implied that men have "property" in their religious opinions, in the liberty and safety of their persons, and in the free use of their physical and mental faculties. When governments pride themselves on guarding the inviolability of property, Madison warned, let them see that they respect the broad property in rights as well as the narrow rights of property. The summing up, however, Madison reserved for an imaginary dialogue between a "Republican" and an "anti-Republican." The latter argues that the government must be strong above all, the people submissive. The Republican expostulates, obviously with Hamilton in mind: "What a perversion of the natural order of things . . . to make power the primary and central object of the social system, and Liberty but its satellite."

In the test by fire which is actual politics rather than political theory, Madison showed himself strong. He distinguished himself first by waging a major campaign against Hamilton's proposal to secure public credit without discriminating in favor of the original holders of the debt. These had been forced to part with their securities at desperately low prices because of the impaired credit under the Articles of Confederation, and the present holders, many of whom were speculators, had bought up the certificates in large quantities after they had discovered that the government, under Hamilton, might honor the securities at face value. Madison's appeal for discrimination between these two classes of holders, based on what he considered equitable and humane, did not succeed in changing Hamilton's plan for securing the public debt. But it showed the sincerity of his stated ideals of moral restraints on the use of power, and it was the beginning of a fateful holding action by Republicans against the Federalists and their broad program of power.

The same issue lies at the heart of the famous controversy over the "strict" and "broad" interpretations of the Constitution. Jefferson and Madison, watching the logically progressive steps taken by Hamilton and the Federalists for tightening their grasp on state power, could hardly feel it safe to agree with Hamilton's axiom that "every power vested in a government is in its nature sovereign, and includes . . . a right to employ all the *means* requisite and fairly applicable to the attainment of the ends of such power. . . ." Madison in an important speech to Congress, and Jefferson in a parallel opinion on the constitutionality of the Federal Bank sent to President Washington at his request, both argued that the phrases "to lay taxes to provide for the general welfare" and "to make all laws necessary and proper for carrying into execution the enumerated powers" could not be used to reduce the whole Constitution to the single statement that Congress be instituted with power to do whatever would be for the good of the United States. For in that event, Jefferson warned, the administration would be the sole judges of good and evil, and thus in fact they would have the power to do whatever evil they pleased. Madison, who well remembered what had taken place in the Convention, recalled that the proposal to authorize Congress to open canals and incorporate them had been rejected for one reason, because it was feared that Congress might then also have the power to create a bank. In the Convention, Madison had proposed that Congress be empowered to "grant charters of incorporation," but the delegates rejected his suggestion. He interpreted this as the intention to confine Congress to the enumerated powers and to the *indispensable* means to carry the enumerated powers into effect. Apart from the intricate arguments advanced by both sides, there were two substantial issues in conflict. Jefferson and Madison were trying to safeguard the people's liberty from what they were now calling a "money despotism," and they were anxious to protect the states in order to have the states as a countervailing power against further national assumptions of power. Hamilton hoped to carry out, by energetic administration, his original ideal of a strong national government, free from what he called the "depredations" of the states and the untrustworthy common people they might represent.

Some years later, in 1798 and 1799, in a crisis situation, Jefferson and Madison issued famous protests against the oppressive Alien and Sedition Laws passed by the Federalists. These were the "Virginia and Kentucky Resolutions," which effectually discouraged the federal government from ever again attempting to move openly against the freedom of the press. Far more was involved than the dialectic of "states' rights" to which the two authors resorted. They were waging a classic fight to defend civil liberties and to keep alive the two-party system without which only the husk of self-government can remain.

Power, then, in one form or another, is necessary to protect liberty. In simplistic fashion this truth becomes distorted by some people into a naïve cult of efficiency, and grave fears are voiced that democracy is weak because it is less organized than total economies. In this mood Hamilton is revered as the symbol of organizing imagination and managerial power. But people forget that it was no mean business to control Hamilton's power, both in Congress, where his fiscal reports were presented, and in the executive, where his power tended to override that of the other Cabinet members. Madison as leader in Congress and Jefferson as Secretary of State were able to curb Hamilton's power program and thereby assure that the Secretary of the Treasury should not have the full executive powers he tried to assume. This aspect of Jefferson's and Madison's realistic efforts to assure limited powers at the outset of our government is not taken into account by those who worship Hamilton as the realist.

3

Madison developed some basic but not obvious implications of this central position at a remarkably early phase in the development of democratic theory. One aspect happens to be older and much sounder than the one normally accepted as the classic British formulation of liberalism, that of John Stuart Mill. Mill's position tends to posit reason at the center of all democratic procedures and to assume a habit or practice of rationality as characteristic of human nature. This view distorts the actual findings about human nature in all societies about which we have knowledge. In order to reject such an undue emphasis on reason, one does not have to ground the rejection on the findings of Freud or the sociological derivative formulation in Pareto's theory of nonlogical actions. For it appears that Madison, without benefit of Freud or Pareto, found it possible to establish a realistic position on human nature as the center of his political theory. He held that men were naturally moved by interests and associated passions and would naturally organize themselves to protect and promote these interests. But men could also respond to the appeal of more important and enduring "general interests," especially if they were helped to do so by being denied a monopoly of power! This is the basic significance of Madison's theory of factions.

This theory of factions, as a proper outcome of the workings of human nature in any society, enabled Madison on important occasions in his career to seize strategic opportunities to promote liberty in a realistic setting. In truth, one should understand that it is this conception of strategic opportunities which distinguishes the work of a philosopher-statesman from that of both a political opportunist and a philosopher-king. The opportunist does not function as a principled political leader; he is not committed to serious moral stakes. The philosopher-king is too far removed from a political setting to have any effective bearing on translating ideal outcomes into directed actions and therefore tends to complain about all society and mankind for refusing to be led to the perfect state. Now, Madison had moral goals—the extension of liberty, not only here and now but over time and, he hoped, over the earth. For this reason he recognized conflicting interests and the need somehow to resolve and compromise these interests while advancing—not sacrificing—the cause of liberty. His work on the separation of church and state, his concern with the separation of powers, the dual sovereignty envisaged in the Constitution, as well as the time limitations upon holding legislative and executive authority, his ultimate sponsorship of the Bill of Rights, and his tireless defense of the Union after sharp North-South conflict had developed in the last years of his life—all these activities recognized the need to work somehow through factional interests to the common good.

The theory of factions has been seized on as a kind of primitive formulation of the theory of class. But here, too, it is important to recognize Madison's advance not only over Mill but also over Marx. Marx's so-called realism amounts to a denial of ideal motives and the reduction of political and other interests to a class position in the economy. This is clearly a serious distortion of human nature and human behavior—not to say of history. Madison recognized the pervasive character of conflict in all human society and the pervasive drive to improve the conditions of society. Marx felt that he was inheriting the mantle of liberalism by espousing the myth of a *classless* society to succeed all political organizations of states which defend class and, ultimately, economic position. There is, according to Madison's understanding of the *universal* character of factional behavior, no possibility of such a leap from political necessity to social freedom. For Marx, the theory of the classless society may not, apparently, have been intended as a noble lie, nor was it the ignoble lie used in Communist propaganda as one weapon among others to force men to accept the current state of tyranny. We must credit Madison's political realism with convicting Marx himself of utopian socialism. What is more, it convicts all utopias of serious political error, because they ignore the reality of factions and posit a more perfect state or society than could possibly be realized. Acting on utopian theory can only result in the assumption of arbitrary and ultimately total power to keep intact the utopian citadel, a confectionary citadel concocted out of an unrealistic view of man.

4

Madison's enlightened realism is presented in unforgettable terms in an unaddressed draft of a letter written late in his life. Madison dryly wrote:

No government of human device and human administration can be perfect; . . . that which is the least imperfect is therefore the best government; that the abuses of all other governments have led to the preference of republican governments as the best of all governments, because the least imperfect.

In short, there is no perfect state. The "idealistic" theory that there is one, is likely to lead to a total state, as in Plato or in Marx. But there is a *best state under the given conditions,* and this is one which permits majority rule while protecting minority rights—essentially, the democratic form of government. And there are always possibilites for more democracy. This enables us to distinguish between the failings of a democracy at any one time or place and the negation of democracy altogether. It is not necessary to deny there is Negro discrimination to affirm there is democracy in the United States.

Another implication of Madison's theory of conjoining power with liberty has some bearing on the current debate on security measures in a democratic society. Power does tend to corrupt, unless it is moved by moral goals and is limited by political safeguards of the kind imposed in the Constitution—regular elections, the separation of powers, and the Bill of Rights, among others. But even then certain interests, when organized politically, may be out to seize power and, when in power, destroy the safeguards for other minorities. Therefore under certain conditions it may be necessary, in order to protect liberty, to use power to prevent such interests from functioning effectively. There is no justification for being so weak as to invite disaster, but there is an exacting obligation to be careful to use only as much power as is necessary to protect liberty. Obviously, conditions will vary at any one time as to whether more or less power is required for this purpose. There will be differences about the extent of the power needed to combat present evils. By the same logic, however, there may be opportunities, for those not moved by moral ends, to seize upon changed situations to strengthen their own power. The guide for Madison in this complex nexus of power and liberty is similar to the guide for Justice Holmes, the test of a "clear and present danger"; and this standard must take into account whether avenues to reason have been kept relatively open or have been blocked.

Two further aspects of the theory of factions in relation to democratic governments are pertinent to contemporary problems. Both these aspects have to do with Madison's belief that the American republic was likely to be more successful than previous experiments because it would be an "extensive" republic. Extension, for Madison, involved the multiplication of factions on the probability that, with the ways open for debate and public discussion, plus the political safeguards established in the Constitution, no one faction would be overwhelming.

We see factions today, organized on a national scale, exercising their influence to secure their self-interest. Yet they do not preclude the coexistence of other factions—in part because they are not overwhelming and in part because they are not wholly unified as a single faction. Agriculture, labor, and business exert combined pressures on the government. The people must choose their government in the light of the issues and programs sponsored by these factions and by other pressure groups, as they are reflected in party platforms and legislative proposals. Clearly, we all need agriculture, labor, and business, and consequently there is no convenient wholesale solution for ridding ourselves of these special interests. There is no doubt that serious national problems have been created by parity pricing, monopolistic labor organizations, or monopolistic business interests and influences. For these reasons our future success as a democracy depends in large part on the wisdom we cultivate in compromising, balancing, and resolving these special interests to promote the cause of liberty. This is one aspect of Madison's theory of factions that has meaning today.

The other aspect of the extensive republic and the multiplication and diffusion of factions concerns Madison's hope that our form of government might function as an inspirational model for the rest of the world. An extensive republic that is best for man, not in being perfect but in being least imperfect, is one that moves toward a world government. This is, so to speak, the goal of man's efforts to use the power he can create to secure peace and freedom. This, in a sense, is the secular equivalent of "peace on earth to men of good will." Drawing up exquisite blueprints of ideal societies or perfect constitutions cannot bring us one step nearer to the goal, nor can the wild suggestion of preventive war set us on the path. Madison's strategy is the only one potentially useful in moving us in this direction. It would imply organizing workable federations of united states where there are joint needs and where tolerable procedures for solving factional issues can be established.

The problems of Western Europe may look hopeless to many today, but so did those of the states under the Articles of Confederation. It was the recognition of strong mutual interests, the spur of self-preservation, and the cogent and disinterested leadership of great Americans that made the Constitutional Convention a success. Europe today may appear to have unsolvable and irreconcilable problems. But there are mutual interests: there is the increasing spur of self-preservation; and there are indications among Europeans of the need for disinterested leadership. And here Madison's hope for the role of America as a catalyst in organizing more extensive republics is not only morally compelling but may perhaps function as a practical guide.

Western Europe, of course, is only one area where the United States is called upon to exercise its influence in organizing the free world. And those who know the radical diversity of other cultures and areas outside the mainstream of Western European civilization despair of all efforts to stimulate the growth of democracy or to further the creation of democratic alliances. What would Madison's counsel suggest here in the toughest area for future statesmanship? I should like to approach this question by what may seem an indirection, a diversion, but what I hope will be addressed squarely to the issue so far as it can be talked about with a modicum of sense.

The significance of this Madisonian view of liberty against power should be apparent today. The leaders of the Soviet Union, on any sustained and close analysis, are not concerned with using power to promote man's freedom but are concerned primarily with assuring the maintenance of their own power. They have been able to conceal this issue by vesting themselves in the trappings of socialist hopes and ideals. They have taken the offensive by claiming that the United States is a corrupt, capitalistic, imperialistic state, whereas they speak for the oppressed of the world and use their power in a world bent upon destroying their position. Their astounding success with this strategy is made clear when those who would oppose them are forced to think in power terms, as the new Machiavellians.

To counter this strategy we must come to see both the vitality of the ideals of liberty and the necessity for using power to promote these ideals. The leaders of the Soviet Union themselves are aware of the hopes engendered by the cause of liberty. This is the meaning of their dialectical double talk, which uses terms like "a people's democracy," "a Soviet Constitution," and "a classless society" to convince the people that they are for peace and democracy. We cannot meet this challenge of ruthless power draped in the folds of liberty and holding the dove of peace without recognizing the real implications of moral ideals. We must not succumb to power against power, to the cynical refusal to promote human ideals because there is a formidable, aggressive power which threatens our freedom and that of the free world—that is, in minimum terms, that part of the world still free from the domination of the Soviet Union or its political hacks. Ideals of liberty still move mankind, and move those countries not yet enslaved to build up the necessary power to negotiate from positions of strength. The philosophy of democracy, in recognizing the joint ties of liberty and power, is not a new propaganda device invented to meet a short-run dilemma, as power propagandists sometimes imply. It is a strong, genuine tradition and has urgent contemporary meaning. Madison is one of the few far-sighted philosopher-statesmen who helped establish and develop this vital tradition.

5

In his time Madison made himself a critic of the kind of institutionalized religion that claimed to have rights over all men to force its particular brand of faith. He affirmed the national right to religious belief along the path which a free conscience has chosen. The source of his faith was a love of man expressed by devotion to the real and solid condition that could encourage men to be fully human—the universal recognition of the equal rights of men to be free, to govern themselves as best they could, to better their physical, social, mental, and spiritual life. Cherishing this faith as one that could unite men and constitute, in effect, a common faith, Madison repudiated every attempt by religious organizations to obtain control in the political domain. For one who sincerely cultivated the equal rights of men, only a republican setting where men would be free to worship—or even not to worship—was fitting. In his own day, therefore, Madison succeeded in the Virginia legislature in establishing religious freedom and separating church and state. He extended this position in the Constitutional Convention and repeated his success in the First Congress by moving for the introduction of the Bill of Rights.

This insistence upon the purely private dimension of religious worship and its attendant warning against any attempted church invasion of the state is familiar to anyone who knows the early history of this country. But it is necessary, nevertheless, to call attention to it today because in our opposition to Communist power there is a tendency to seek some other total salvation. It is right, in Madison's terms, to attack the Communist philosophy as a false totalitarian faith, one which denies the natural rights of man. But there is, according to the founding fathers, no justification for forcing the belief that there is one and only one true religion for all, by which all other ways of life and belief are to be cried down as false and wiped out.

By this, as indeed by all his hard struggles, Madison was declaring his great faith in the uniqueness of the American system, that "federative" system which he loved and proudly described as "itself not a little experimental. . . . It not only excites emulation without enmity, but admits local experiments of every sort, which, if failing, are but a partial and temporary evil; if successful, may become a common and lasting improvement." This was the Madison who had ruefully reflected in the *Federalist Papers* that men were not angels and that government itself is "the greatest of all reflections of human nature. If men were angels, no government would be necessary. If angels were to govern men, neither external nor internal controls on government would be necessary." By such realistic judgments accompanied by a generous faith in man, Madison was recommending, I would think, the positive encouragement of variety in unity. No one religion, he saw, could unite society or mankind—one political state, or way of life, or mental set. Yet all men could have one common faith, as common as their existence as natural animals, as common as their need for air, for food, for movement from place to place, for borrowing and improving each other's ideas. That faith—one that could spread by exciting "emulation without envy," that experiment that would touch off similar but not identical experiments, that growing unity that could be worked from the most diverse materials—that was the faith in the natural rights of man. It was and is a powerful faith, that none monopolize, no nation owns, and no one can be diminished by.

We can easily understand how one who had translated such a high faith into a unique political experiment, a "workshop of liberty," would take pride, as he looked back over a half-century, that "the ark" had survived. Such deeply engrained hopes and love moved Madison to leave a last message to his countrymen—a message which has assuredly not lost its meaning for our divided world. This message solemnly states:

As this advice, if it ever see the light will not do it till I am no more, it may be considered as issuing from the tomb, when the truth alone can be respected, and the happiness of man alone consulted. It will be entitled therefore to whatever weight can be derived from good intentions, and from the experiences of one who has served his country in various stations through his life to the cause of its liberty and who has borne a part in most of the transactions which will constitute epochs of its destiny.

The advice nearest to my heart and deepest in my convictions is that the Union of the States be cherished and perpetuated. Let the open enemy to it be regarded as a Pandora with her box opened; and the disguised one, as the serpent creeping with his deadly wiles into Paradise.

CHAPTER VII

The Idea of America

PROBABLY the phrase "the idea of America" is open to grave misunderstanding. It may be misunderstood to mean that the "idea" is single—that our national history represents the unfolding of one irrevocable idea, somewhat after the pattern of the Hegelian dialectic. This notion is quite false. There is no single "correct" idea that can sum up the multiple and in some cases contradictory aspects of American life and American history. A plurality of ideas, as well as of national origins, customs, and religions, exists in the American community and defies synthesis into some "higher" unity.

Consider in this connection some of the more important ideas that have been associated with America: America is the land of toleration and equality, but it is also the land where racial discrimination, often accompanied by violence, robs certain minority groups of their constitutional rights. America is the land open to the oppressed of the world, but it is often symbolized as exploitative or imperialist—remember "The Big Stick" and "The Yankee Dollar." It is the land where men are believed to be educable and therefore capable of self-government, but it is also the land where corruption and crime flourish and where racketeers sometimes associate with and control politicians. It is the land of generous policies, of hospitality, but

others often see us as a land of bossiness and brag. It is the land
of personal liberty, of informality in manners, of freely changing morals and behavior. Alas, it is also the land where a New
England township stoned a man, in the last century, because he
dared to wear a beard when the rest of his townsmen were beard-
less. It is a land as avid for "pull," as crass in measuring men by
their possessions, as more mannered societies ever were or could
be. The point is that American virtues rarely come pure. There
are accompanying vices. And if we are not universally loved or
even substantially appreciated when we think we deserve it,
there are reasons for our impaired popularity.

There is, then, so single idea that correctly portrays the American development; there is no inevitable "march" to our history.
We are not part of a wave of the future, nor are we assured that
our "destiny" will delight us. What we are and will become is
not independent of our united conduct; our history has been
and still is the outcome of our own individual efforts. It is important to clear away the remaining wisps of Hegelian fog at
a time when the moral choices and long-range decisions that we
ourselves make will steer us through the troubled future—or
nothing will.

Yet our history and our tradition do present ideas and ideals
which are distinctively American and which, if we choose to
advance them, may serve as operating models in helping us to
realize a great idea—that man can make his history so that he
will be free to realize his best nature. In this sense there are indeed aspects of the American tradition which we may select to
emphasize the more enduring and the better qualities of American endeavor and which can serve to guide us in the future.

1

We are now close to using the word "idea" in the phrase "the
idea of America" to refer to an ideal or a set of ideals. Such usage
is particularly appropriate to the American experience, for it
is a fact that America was conceived in thought before it came

to be. That thought had an ideal aspect in the hope nourished by the early settlers that, if they built well, the new wilderness would become "Earth's only Paradise," where every man could live by his lights, free of temporal and spiritual dictation. As John Adams correctly expressed it, in eulogizing the spirit of the early Pilgrim separatists and Puritan dissenters, the settlement of America should not be attributed to "religion alone, as is commonly supposed; but . . . [to] a love of universal liberty, and a hatred, a dread, a horror" of tyranny. In line with this ideal the early colonizers began that long process of working out a new pattern of society, shaping it first to provide for their own religious freedom and then, led on by the challenge of new conditions, undertaking further social experimentation.

The cynical may object that those who settled here for religious freedom did not concede it very readily to others who differed with them. It is true that soon the holy commonwealths settled into rigid theocracies, and that a part of New England moved far from the vital faith of the Pilgrim and Puritan fathers, becoming a busy market place and pausing (as one critic has put it) only "every seventh day to wear its Sunday halo." But the logic of the attitude that one should worship according to one's lights, in tune with the spiritual truth independently arrived at by reading the Bible, could not be contained. Against the theocratic Mathers and John Cottons arose the Anne Hutchinsons and Roger Williamses. Whether they were fundamentally more spiritual and more tolerant is unimportant. It suffices that they were different, and were prepared to fashion communities anew on the principle that differences should be tolerated.

The cynical may further object to treating America as an ideal, pointing out that the ranks of the colonizers were swelled by bonded servants, criminals, debtors—the poor who hoped for greater security and the middle class who hoped for greater prestige. Were these conglomerated groups in any way attached to America as the promise of a better world to be won? Yes, if only in the mundane and everyday sense that they would be getting rid of intolerable or restrictive conditions in the Old World at the price of some personal courage and hard work in the New. To these people too—except, of course, those who were shanghaied into the land of liberty—America meant a fresh start, a better chance for bread, a freer world than they had ever known.

To hold an ideal is one thing; to work it out is another. If the first phase of the ideal of America was largely fashioned in religious terms, the second was more secular and more mixed. A new country had to be built up from the ground in accord with desirable goals, and the goals were modified by the objective conditions which confronted the builders. This is the nature of an experiment, where ideas guide activity to test certain conclusions and reach intended outcomes. As colonial experience accumulated, men who were encouraged by an apparently limitless new continent began to think of themselves as a new breed—Americans. The firmer the hold the colonials established on the continent, the better their cultivation of the fields became, the more their ships rode out to the West Indies, the East, and the shores of Europe, and the farther west the adventurous probed—into the Ohio territory and Illinois, running the risk of warfare with Indian tribes—the stronger grew the faith of the individual American in his own competence and his own country. An elixir was at work on American colonials. They saw life full of opportunities and believed they were alive under a *new* sky.

This was the American, that "new man" whom Crèvecoeur hailed in his enthusiastic letters abroad. Americans, he vowed, acted upon new principles; they had new ideas and opinions— all suited to the unique new country where they resided. Tocqueville carried this thought further, describing the new society as "the great experiment." "In that land," he wrote, "the great experiment of the attempt to construct society upon a new basis was to be made by civilized man; and it was there, for the first time, that theories hitherto unknown, or deemed impracticable, were to exhibit a spectacle for which the world had not been prepared by the history of the past." This is a key phrase, "the great experiment." It accounts for the earnestness and intensity with which Americans in the era of the young republic sought to make their new democracy work. They felt that the rights of man prospered or fell, depending upon what happened here. If men could successfully be treated as adults in society and in politics, then governments that dealt with them as children, puppets, ciphers, or slaves were doomed.

2

The classic formulation of the ideals to which the great experiment was dedicated appears in the Declaration of Independence. The inalienable rights there invoked, as everyone knows, are the rights to life, liberty, and the pursuit of happiness, and the ground for these "inalienable" rights is proclaimed as the "self-evident" belief that all men are created equal.

Since this principle of equality is the heart of the social philosophy contained in the Declaration, it would be sensible to decide what is meant by it, and whether it remains a valid ideal for modern society. In one sense all Americans claim to accept the idea of equality. But when one studies the wide range of attitudes and values included under the same verbal symbol, one despairs of the meaning of the term.

We might start to fix the meaning of the principle of equality by taking note of the fact that Jefferson, the apostle of equality, wrote with conviction about the existence of a "natural aristocracy." Men were plainly unequal, Jefferson held, in talents, abilities, moral discipline, and practical genius. He firmly believed that if education were made accessible to all, many inequalities of an environmental and accidental sort would be reduced, though never eliminated. He thought it desirable to provide conditions that would permit merit to determine each man's different (unequal) station in life. John Adams went even further in exchanges with Jefferson on this point. He maintained that it is not desirable to act as if one could remove chance inequalities. Each man, he thought, should struggle against them as best he could. There would be greater zest to social relations and a richer variety of personalities in a community where family traditions, property, wealth, and prestige played a part than in one where all men were reduced to an undifferentiated, lower common denominator. On this issue, Adams was, as usual, intelligently conservative, and Jefferson was, as usual, intelligently liberal. Jefferson, who had far stronger claims to personal membership in an aristocratic class than John Adams, resented those who acquired power without commensurate merit, distrusted those who valued power in itself, and despised a community that prevented impoverished young people from acquiring all the knowledge that civilized institutions of learning could give them.

Equality, then, is not of status or origin, but of opportunity, of moral and political rights. Jefferson and Adams (together with Franklin and the others who made up the Committee on the Declaration of Independence) were not simply *describing* a fact about human nature. They were *prescribing* the policy that would allow man to realize human nature as fully as possible. Franklin, who had made himself into a successful businessman and diplomat; Adams, who had worked for his place as an American leader by a rigorous career at law and municipal politics and by hard application to the study of history and political theory; Jefferson, who had broken free of the narrow concerns of a plantation owner and the party-going gaieties of a well-born young Virginian to become a serious lawyer, a tireless legislator, and an inspired statesman—they all had a very sharp impression of qualitative differences in men, even in those who had been given equal opportunities for education and for public service.

Economically, equality does not mean that there must be uniformity of living conditions or equal compensation for socially useful work. Those who cherish the principle of equality should aim to provide for two requirements: that none should be deprived of the necessities of life in order to provide luxuries for a few and that conditions should be devised to promote equalization rather than sharp differentiation. Politically, the doctrine of equality does not forbid men to be leaders, but it does demand that leaders merit their eminence. It further insists that men are equal in the sense that government should be based upon their freely given consent and that it should be bound by limiting devices framed to prevent the power-hungry from capturing dictatorial powers. Socially and personally, the principle of equality implies something akin to the Kantian imperative that all men be treated as ends, never merely as means, and the Christian belief in the infinite worth of the human personality. Throughout this wide range of meaning one finds a single assumption about the principle of equality: if men are treated in some essential respects as though they were equals, in a community to which they actively belong, they are likely to become better than if they were treated otherwise. This is a moral assumption and therefore compelling, but it is also completely realistic.

3

All this was aptly stated in fresh terms by another of America's true philosopher-statesmen. James Madison, in philosophic retirement, with a wealth of extraordinary scholarship and experience behind him, defined the role of America in a little-known letter to a friend. He wrote:

The free system of government we have established is so congenial with reason, with common sense, and with a universal feeling, that it must produce approbation and a desire of imitation. . . . Our country, if it does justice to itself, will be the officina-Libertatis [workshop of liberty], to the Civilized World, and do more than any other for the uncivilized.

In this revelatory phrase, "workshop of liberty," the sage thinker who earned himself the title "Father of the Constitution" crystallized the dynamic meaning of "the idea of America." Here work and liberty are explicitly connected. America must work to achieve a free society. And the labor envisaged is not that of isolated individuals but is, rather, part of an orderly and organized workshop, where workers together produce useful objects. Nor is liberty free, like the air—a property man is endowed with or a country "the home of" through a stroke of luck. It is something that must be established by men who cherish it and maintained by a society that concedes its value.

Moreover, the workshop is a symbol of technology, and technology is devised to lighten man's innumerable burdens. In the long run technology flourishes most in a society based on free inquiry, a society that zealously guards the intellectual freedom of its thinkers and scientists. Though it is clear that even such a society is forced, in times of national peril, to place responsible limits on governmental personnel and on the diffusion of scientific information to achieve security, the security restrictions which hedge certain current technological developments must be short-run limitations wrung from a democratic community for purposes of self-preservation. They must not become fundamental denials of the value or ideal of intellectual freedom in the republic where the pursuit of human happiness remains the declared objective of social organization.

Critics may stigmatize America's technological good fortune as machine worship or power worship, but they have missed the point. The control of machines for liberty, for bettering man's estate, follows as a natural and logical consequence from the explicit intentions of Jefferson, Madison, and their associates to recognize the adult nature of citizens in a republic. Not only were free citizens to cherish political liberty and work to maintain it, they were also to be trained in the informal practice of science. In short, they were to be devoted to the experimental method of seeking truth, and this was the basis for expecting "reasonable" men, "reasonable" actions, "reasonable" compromises. In this sense the great American experiment was suffused through and through with the spirit of controlled experimentation. If every man was to be a king to the extent that he shared the supreme political power once considered a hereditary monopoly, every man was also to be a scientific spirit sharing in the search for experimental truth. This is the reason that the founding fathers were so much concerned with popular education and the study of history. History was valued in a special way as the laboratory where human relations had been tried and had partially failed or partially succeeded.

While the phrase "workshop of liberty" must be understood in this broad social sense, it must also be taken in a more literal way to mean America's original role as the beacon to the oppressed of all countries who seek work in freedom. Those who have come here as immigrants in various epochs of this nation's past have recognized that, however arduous work may be, it is lightened and becomes meaningful when it is freely chosen and when it can be viewed as a contribution to the sharable total product—particularly when increasing that sharable total product repays the worker by increasing leisure and raising the standard of living. Because America joins work with liberty in this practical way, there has been growing clamor on the part of people not so free to gain entry here. This is still the country the world's oppressed would choose if they had a choice; the knowledge that America is the workshop of liberty still makes a difference to people the world over—fortunately, for it is this America that alone can contend with the society of the concentration camp and slave labor.

It is the workshop of liberty that makes possible the "pursuit of happiness." That felicitous phrase has not been appreciated in all its strength because it is often wrongly understood to mean the pursuit of some series of pleasures, and from that interpretation it is only a step to the allegation that this is a materialistic culture. On the contrary, the pursuit of happiness is rather to be taken in the Aristotelian sense—a sense that Jefferson fully understood and intended—implying the happiness appropriate to the human condition, substantial happiness that is achieved by the mature development of man's fullest potentialities.

This union of America's individualistic ideal, the pursuit of happiness, with the primary function of American society, to be a workshop of liberty, provides a basis for understanding the American idea. Only an open society, like the American, can provide the conditions for the fullest realization of every individual's capacities. Only an environment of intellectual freedom, political criticism, trial and error, and the self-correction that flows from them can come to terms with man's inquiring mind and inventive spirit. Only a society that values the people who compose it can properly protect them—ensuring them freedom from want without denying them a large area of choice in values and conduct. To the extent that America has achieved something of the quality of an open society, it has made good on the promissory phrase, "the rights of man."

4

These aspects of the American idea and experience have an intellectual counterpart in the conception of man as a "tool-making animal" (as Benjamin Franklin called him) and in the developed philosophy of science and democracy which the greatest of American philosophers—from Thomas Jefferson to John Dewey—have made their distinctive work. America's version of this philosophy has variously been called "pragmatism," "instrumentalism," "naturalism," "experimentalism"; but it may be usefully summed up under the last of these labels. For the joining of republican or democratic theory with free inquiry is crystallized in a phrase that has more than historic interest—it is a deliberate proposal to view the initial programs that might turn us in the direction of democratic society as "the American experiment." The term "experiment" implies systematic investigation guided by an idea or hypothesis, rather than random activity. It suggests organized social inquiry in a setting which recognizes that everyone shares, in some degree, the supreme political power. It envisages the resolution of political problems in a social environment of intellectual freedom, criticism, trial and error, and a continuing process of self-correction. Moreover, the resort to an unusual term like "experiment" applied to political theory was, in its time, eloquent of the severe critical judgments these republican theorists made of nondemocratic governments and societies. They dared to advocate the hypothesis that democratic society would honor human freedom more, on the grounds that the monarchies, aristocracies, and dictatorships that they knew, or knew about, had blatantly and decisively employed power in the interest of an elite, a special class, or for aggressive wars, at the expense of "the most numerous class" in society, the people. Their uncompromising rejection of the evil of concentrated power and the easy transition from it to tyranny provided all the stimlus they needed to try to formulate a political form that would promote human freedom.

For one implication of the experimental hypothesis about the functioning of a democratic state, consider the assumptions implicit in the Constitution. Made explicit, they might be read: All men are fallible and likely to blunder because of their failure of knowledge or their lack of objectivity face to face with issues that affect them closely. Let us limit the extent of their blunders; and, above all, let us keep open the channels by which their blunders can be pointed out, explored, and condemned. Let us also see to it that the blunderers will be replaced, in due course, by other men, who will in their turn compose the government temporarily. Some of the past blunders will be corrected and some better courses instituted. There is no magic calculus in this procedure; men are attaining political improvement the hard way, the way of the intelligently controlled experiment appropriate to the workshop of liberty.

5

A second implication of the hypothesis about the functioning of a democratic state concerns the content of the politics of freedom. A variety of philosophical traditions has endowed "freedom" with such diverse connotations that, for instance, obedience to authority and freedom to choose and act "as one pleases, without any restraint" have both been claimed as its definitive properties. Worse still, we have heard the theory, and seen the results, of "forcing men to be free." It is therefore a prime responsibility for anyone who is interested in defending human freedom to stipulate the essential conditions without which we have an unfree, nondemocratic society. I believe the formulation of a theory of republican government which specifies these essential conditions is the significance of the work of the founding fathers. They indicated that the minimal conditions of freedom, those by which we may test whether a given society is free and the extent to which it is free, are four—equality of consideration under the law; majority consent for the government; freedom of inquiry; and freedom of choice, subject to the other conditions.

The first essential test, equal treatment under the law, is the principle of justice and involves a society that is structured with some degree of order and recognized "liberties." This is a precondition for the other conditions of freedom, since it is adherence to this principle that provides reasonable security of life. As an explicit declaration, one can equate it roughly to the famous Thirty-ninth Article of the Magna Carta, which, of course, provides that "no free man shall be taken or imprisoned . . . or in any way destroyed . . . except by the lawful judgment of his peers or the law of the land." In the intervening history of seven-hundred years the common civil rights associated with this principle add to the basic stipulation that the law is no respecter of persons the prohibitions against arbitrary arrest, detention, or exile; the right to fair trial before an impartial tribunal; and freedom from arbitrary interference with one's privacy, home, or family. Violation of this first condition is characteristic of modern totalitarianism and in itself definitive of political slavery—where the rule of force can resort to mass murder, arbitrary imprisonment, and the invasion of every privacy without fear that the destruction worked on a man will involve the possibility of redress under equal and impartial law. Thus, the function of this first condition is to give political significance to "the right to life."

The second condition, the consent of the governed under some standard approximating majority rule, provides for the freedom to influence the equal and impartial law under which we live. The right of all adults to participate in the government must be given operational reality, at least in terms of regular elections, at stated intervals, and in a situation of real choice—that is, where the voter may choose from at least two candidates and where there are at least two opposing parties. "Majority rule" may indeed be subject to the charge of theoretical vagueness or literal inexactness in certain selected decisions of a democratic electorate, but in principle it has served, and can serve, as an impediment to elitist and despotic government and as a positive directional standard to which progressives and reformers may repair when government begins to cut free of a high degree of control or influence by the people.

The third condition is related to the second, but broader. It is the freedom to explore all alternatives—which can only mean the freedom to inquire, to think, to speak, to write—so long as one does not seriously endanger the lives of others. This condition illuminates the political significance of "the right to liberty."

The fourth condition, the freedom to choose, concerns the manner of life of individuals. The range of choice can be wide in some contexts and relatively narrow in others, but there must be some real choice about the individual's occupation, enjoyments, and so on, subject only to the other conditions. It is "the right to the pursuit of happiness."

It is obvious that all four conditions are interrelated. It should be equally obvious that no absolute freedom has been invoked. There are degrees of freedom, depending on the situation, resources, and overriding problems of the time and also depending on the extent to which the above four conditions are realized. Thus, one other essential truth, which is appropriate in referring to democracy as an "experiment," is the obvious fact that an experiment can fail, and that the process of trial and error that it invokes is not one that calls for a perfected or rigid ideal. It is wholly consistent with a democratic experiment that there will be degrees of democratic realization and degrees of democratic failure. The development of a society organized by democratic political institutions can move in a democratic direction or, in a more or less serious way, in a direction away from democracy. Difficult as it may be to demarcate, without a margin of theoretical dispute, what separates a "democratic" from a "nondemocratic" society, the problem cannot be sidestepped and clearly relates to the defense of freedom as the end and standard of political action.

6

Nobody has ever won tolerance, no nation has ever become an open society without working for it. We have partly had to *earn* our good fortune; let us recall this when we doubt ourselves. But when outsiders doubt America, let us recall the large element of luck that went into the making of our continental riches and our eminence in the world today. We would do well to admit the mistakes and the blemishes in our open society, the blunders out of which we have caught each other up and somehow remedied things in a series of imperfect but useful compromises. The old rule that those who seek pleasure do not find it and those who assume virtue rarely possess it loses none of its force when applied to the American community. America's leadership in the world today can hardly delight a Europe that considers itself not only older but infinitely wiser. When Toynbee, some years back, called America a "semi-barbarian superstate of the cultural periphery," he was saying in sesquipedalian language what he recently said more rudely when he coined the slogan, "No annihilation without representation." The British community is akin to ours as no other is, and if British intellectuals repreat Toynbee's slogan with approval today it is a quick index to the fact that not even Marshall Plan aid suffices to make America universally approved in Europe.

In the Middle East, the Far East, and Latin America the problem of our reputation is far more acute; it grows out of the almost incurable suspicion and hostility of a vastly underprivileged population who regard even benevolent American projects as new menaces of local-joined-with-American exploitation. To try to persuade these populations that they should form a friendly moral community with the privileged people of the United States and to imply that they will win "free enterprise" and "plenty" if they emulate us, is an ignorant and unsightly proposal. Local reforms in countries with large underprivileged populations might depart widely from the economic pattern of a capitalist democracy like America's and still be extremely helpful to those countries. It would be a mistake, then, to assume that encouraging social and political freedom in backward countries means a literal transplantation of American methods and "the American way of life." We must recognize that democratic reform exists whenever steps are taken to narrow the gap between an impoverished populace and fabulously wealthy rulers.

Today America can survive as a workshop of liberty only by importing critical materials from many foreign countries. Because our vast industrial plant must have such materials as chrome, manganese, tungsten, tin, rubber, cobalt, copper, and wool, we depend on the outside world. Surely it is not a large step from the exchange of goods to the exchange of skills, from the exchange of industrial or agricultural methods to the exchange of ideas and values. All forms of friendly communication should be heartily increased.

In dealing with countries less happily situated, America

should honor that part of her tradition that has pointed up the reliability of enlightened self-interest. Not power alone, not force and fraud, nor a wholly altruistic charity should characterize our foreign relations. "What will you get out of your development program?" asked a Middle Eastern king of the American Minister who was pressing a Point Four proposal. "Nothing," replied the American Minister. The king dismissed him and the project instantly. Obviously nothing that generous could be real. He wanted none of it. America is too young, in the eyes of the world, and too lucky to dare to offer charity or to pretend to be disinterestedly generous. We have always been somewhat short on imaginative sympathy and sensitivity in dealing with others. These qualities, if cultivated, would be an inestimable psychological addition to our sound belief in the democratic experiment and in our role as the workshop of liberty.

CHAPTER VIII

Toward an American Philosophy

THE idea of an American philosophy is inescapably bound up with American history. Because this is so, and because I am advocating a more conscious partnership between American history and American philosophy, I want to make plain the assumptions that underlie my point of view. I consider these truths to be virtually self-evident: that the United States is one of the two greatest powers in the world today; that what we do will affect not only our own survival but the fate of Western civilization as well; that men fighting for freedom are moved by great ideals; and that, for these reasons, it is urgent that we see ourselves and that others see us as acting in accord with ideas and ideals which are sharable and worthy of respect.

Fundamental ideas and ideals, when critically formulated and held, constitute a kind of philosophy. Can we identify a distinctive philosophy in the American grain which we might reasonably expect to win approval from others and to which we can give our intelligent loyalty? This should be a philosophy which uses voice and speech natural to Americans. It should reflect an ethos which accepts what we know of man's nature and man's needs. And it must provide a program of strategic ideals—by which I mean ideals rooted in actual circumstances and directed toward the best improvement of man's estate that can be made. Such a philosophy would, in effect, imply a program intent upon achieving a workable balance between personal happiness and growth, on the one hand, and associated sharing and strength, on the other.

It is one thing to say that we need such an American philosophy and another to say that it exists. To establish its existence is precisely the point where philosophy and history must welcome each other and join hands. But there are initial hurdles to be surmounted. American philosophers do not generally concede that there are any great ideas or worthy ideals that are distinctively American and thus, properly speaking, an American philosophic tradition. When they go beyond the bare denial of the fact that there is an American philosophy worthy of notice, they maintain that what there is, is only a weak branch of the great European tree. I must confess that while American history has won its place in American higher education, American philosophy has still to fight its academic battles; and that where it has won, it has won only in a Pickwickian sense—as a humiliating concession to the facts of national life.

Meanwhile, the historians have generally failed to explore the philosophic bearings of the American experience. As a result foreign critics and even native intellectuals see America as lacking in perspective and in spirit. They consider American history a dull, unimaginative affair. Or, worse yet, they surrender to the clichés of caricature—the familiar Mr. Moneybags, for instance, who is to be despised for his inner emptiness, or a four-flushing salesman who says more than he means (like the Near Eastern date vendor, who cried of his wares: "Hassan's dates are larger than they are!"). This is because American history has been either narrowly factual or unwittingly receptive to the backwash of historical materialism. Indeed, how much American history in the first half of this century invited such an interpretation because it was, in a sense, Operation Dustbowl?

In part, of course, America has been subjected to extensive caricature because of the deliberate propaganda of doctrinaire Marxists and the Communist culture troops the world over. Nevertheless, both historians and philosophers share some measure of responsibility because of their common failure to account for and advance the positive aspects of the American experience. I grant that this experience is not uniform, that it includes elements which warrant both caricature and opposition. But surely there is something more that makes our history an experiment in democracy. Have historians and philosophers, for the most part, understood well enough the significance of this American experiment and, if so, why have they not been able to translate it into effective and moving terms? Of course, it is simpler to detect what is wrong in the conventional approach to the American tradition than to point the way to a better one. Perhaps there are several better ways than those we already know. I can only assume the task of speaking honestly for the way which appears right in my own judgment. The richest resource for this reformulation lies, paradoxically, in the province of the historians.

I am referring to the work of the founding fathers. I think that either we have been too apologetic about their work as philosophers or we have effectively buried their work in clichés; and this is substantially true even after a lively decade of historical investigation of this phase of our past. How otherwise can we account for the singularly small impression they have made not only on European writers but on American philosophers? How explain the fact that the best history of political theory by an American philosopher (George Sabine) does not devote a single page to their work? One reason for this may be the fact that they were politicians. This circumstance obscures their double role as thinkers and statesmen, a conjunction which made me years back employ the term "philosopher-statesmen." As statesmen, they had the ability to exercise political leadership; as philosophers, they had a vision of what was desirable. Another reason for ignoring them may be the fact that their thought was communicated largely through correspondence rather than in formal philosophical treatises. Finally, they were influenced by the political philosophers of the Western tradition, so that when their work is noticed at all, it is quickly disposed of as fragmentary and derivative. But this ignores the quality of their formulation of the philosophy of democracy— actually a formulation that is much more thoroughgoing and subtle than that of their predecessors. For their philosophy was an unprecedented effort to explore the practical and theoretical issues raised by the critical problems of the new experiment in self-government.

I think it is understandable why, if professional philosophers have been blind to the philosophical significance of this effort, the historians should be timid in recognizing the treasures of philosophic material that lay within their grasp. Bacon was sage in pointing out that history without intellectual history is "as the statue of Polyphemus with his eye out." But American philosophers and American historians missed the point. The professional philosophers lacked imagination about the homely things which Socrates, under a clear Athenian sky, would have shrewdly and closely observed, while historians failed to catch the genuine accents of an earlier American age, in all its eloquent and reflective informality.

1

These essays have presented my own grounds for regarding the work of these philosopher-statesmen as the greatest contribution we have made to the philosophy of democracy. As I have tried to show, the core of their political philosophy is the conjunction of power with liberty. Power without liberty is tyranny, a perversion of the natural and desirable order of things. A government formed on such a base is doomed to failure because it is eternally at war with the rights of mankind. On the other hand, liberty without power is utopian. A government formed on such a view is also doomed to fail, being unequal to the task of sustaining the equal rights of men. This is why the philosopher-statesmen jointly promoted a strong, but certainly not total, government to succeed the Confederation —a government based on the sovereignty of the people and on deliberate and prudent limitations of power.

Together the philosopher-statesmen developed the far-reaching implications of their major premise that power must be conjoined with liberty. By grasping these implications, we may effectively combat the errors of the political theories that are most influential today. One theory is associated with the classic formulation of liberalism by John Stuart Mill, which made individual liberty a moral absolute, even at the expense of power. Mill defended the right of the individual to make any and every preachment against government. This defense of unlimited freedom of thought and speech is usually assumed to be identical with the position held, for example, by Jefferson and Madison. For like Mill, they defended magnificently the right to heresy and held that truth, left free to compete in the market place, would eventually vanquish error. But unlike Mill, they opposed the right of conspiracy, the right of men to abuse their liberty of thought and speech by destroying liberty itself. Jefferson recognized that truth "by human interposition could be disarmed of her natural weapons, free argument and debate." He therefore reflected that, "perhaps, the single thing which may be required to others, before toleration to them, would be an oath that they would allow toleration to others."

In his essay on liberty, Mill championed individual liberty against democratic government. He had come to distrust and then to despise what he considered the tyranny of the majority, upon whose consent democratic government must rest. He ended by reposing his confidence in the aristocrat of intelligence, the qualified person who should count for more than one in democratic society. Jefferson, Madison, and Adams defended democratic government as the best protector of individual liberty. They warned that men in power are wolves, that they like to feed on sheep, that their nature must be softened, their cunning be contained; further, that power may corrupt even honest and benevolent men who find their way to public office, and that, therefore, ultimate power must rest with the majority of the people, whose common sense and continual vigilance can alone protect them from tyranny. They believed that men are ambitious, vindictive, and rapacious, that they are naturally swayed by diverse interests and passions, that they will organize themselves into different factions to protect and promote their special interests, and that, therefore, democratic government must be established to check and balance the conflict of factions.

2

The other influential political theory of our time is associated with Marx and Engels, who made economic necessity and power the substance of history, denying the reality of liberty itself. They reduced all human activity and choice, all ideals and ideas, to ideological forms of the material transformation of the economic conditions of production. They viewed all government as one class oppressing the majority of the people, democratic government as the economic dictatorship of the capitalist class. Moreover, they argued that the violent seizure of capitalist means of production by the workers would, after a time, make possible the leap from historical necessity to human freedom.

The founding fathers provide more than enough ammunition to blast this philosophy, which sees history as bloody, with economic tooth and claw. There *is* political choice and therefore no universal economic necessity. Marx and Engels were not realists insofar as they failed to recognize the reality of ideals and the pervasive drive of men to improve their own conditions. Furthermore, there is the never-ceasing conflict of factions in society and therefore no classless society. Paradoxical as it may sound, Marx and Engels could themselves be called utopian socialists for their myth of the classless society.

While there is no classless society, nor a perfect state, there is, in Madison's words, "a least imperfect government." The necessary condition for this strategic ideal is the democratic form, a government which derives its power from the people and is administered by persons holding office for a limited period on the basis of free majority consent. The philosopher-statesmen help us to distinguish clearly between the necessary condition for, and the degrees of, democracy. This distinction is useful when we try to pierce the dialectical smokescreen put up by those who fight under the banner of Marx and Engels today. Their reiteration of the term "people's democracy" to describe their totalitarian satellites demonstrates the vital appeal of the democratic form of government the world over, while their attack upon what they term the "dictatorships" of the West simply points up the need to improve the conditions of democracy here and now.

Jefferson summed up the philosophy of democracy in his eightieth year, writing, as he said, "with two crippled wrists, but hurried sometimes beyond the sense of pain":

We believed . . . that man was a rational animal, endowed by nature with rights, with an innate sense of justice; that he could be restrained from wrong and protected in right, by moderate powers, confided to persons of his own choice, and held to their duties by dependence on his own will. We believed that the complicated organization of kings, nobles, and priests, was not the wisest nor the best to effect the happiness of associated man; that wisdom and virtue were not hereditary; that the trappings of such a machinery, consumed by their expense, those earnings of industry they were meant to protect and, by the inequalities they produced, exposed liberty to sufferance. We believed that men, enjoying in ease and security the full fruits of their own industry, enlisted by all their interests on the side of law and order, habituated to think for themselves, and to follow their reason as their guide, would be more easily and safely governed, than with minds nourished in error, and vitiated and debased . . . by ignorance, indigence and oppression. The cherishment of the people then was our principle.

On such grounds Jefferson saw the American experiment as an "Empire for Liberty," and Madison as a "Workshop of

Liberty." These phrases are both reminders that liberty is not, as it was for Plato, a perfect archetype in the heavens but a hard-won compromise, a strategic ideal. The American philosopher-statesmen dared to hope that this unique and novel experiment would prosper and win a lasting good for mankind, that it might, indeed, become a model for similar experiments elsewhere, accommodated always to variations in native genius and circumstance.

3

The democratic philosophy of the founding fathers is not simply an episode or accident but the touchstone of the American philosophic tradition. The founding fathers are by no means alone in American history in their interest in and their prophetic vision of the possibilities inherent in the American experiment. There are many Americans who made a contribution. Of these, I can mention only a few. One phase of the tradition is implicit in the faith of the English dissenters who came to this country to fashion a new world closer to their conception of a free man's place to worship. But it was Benjamin Franklin, with his enlightened benevolence, frankly secular morality, spontaneous encouragement of education, and genius for experimentation, who was, in Jefferson's phrase, the "father of American philosophy."

After the philosopher-statesmen we move to the world of literary philosophy, to Ralph Waldo Emerson. What Emerson contributed to the American tradition was the perspective of moral individualism, the literary explication of what it means to live as a courageous, value-choosing person engaged in a complex world, as well as the suggestion that American intellectuals must never again commit the sin of pride, founded on ignorance of others and puffed up by naïve self-appreciation. Once the romantic haze of mid-nineteenth-century New England had evaporated, American philosophy came into its own, in the hands of the professional philosophers—notably Charles

Sanders Peirce and William James. Whether their pragmatism be despised as a low utilitarianism or revered as an experimental humanism, it is in fact the major American contribution to professional philosophy, crystallizing the human meaning of modern experimental science.

In our own time this tradition flowered in the work of the late John Dewey. Dewey brought to fulfillment in our world the basic American affirmation of the individual person as the bearer of human values. He associated freedom and democracy with experimental science. He made explicit every American's debt to Western civilization by mastering the work of his predecessors in order to bring their insights to bear on the problems of contemporary man and society. Those who preferred to worship and embalm the great philosophers were irate with Dewey's method. Convinced that they found the key to eternal truths in selected classic texts, they were angered at Dewey's presumption that philosophy needed reconstruction. Dewey's main effort was directed toward the reconstruction of philosophy in order to make human and social experience richer and more complete. Impressed with the fact of generation rather than the myth of eternity, Dewey showed that human experience is continuous with nature and that the scientific method, as the most successful exercise in human intelligence, is capable of resolving human problems and advancing the human estate. But Dewey never made of science a thing to be worshiped. It was simply the most valuable tool of inquiry that human beings had devised, and it was now high time to apply that method in the interests of life, liberty, and the pursuit of happiness. It is worth remarking that John Dewey, alone among the great philosophers, had no qualms about Jefferson's philosophic status and that he did not hesitate to labor at rounding out ideas and ideals already at home in the American tradition. His instrumentalism should be understood for what it is—homespun, congenial to native experience, and yet, in its humane and scholarly way, a valuable perspective wherever men adore freedom and the life of purpose and mind. In Dewey, the representative American philosopher, we see philosophy as the ever-human task of attempting to enrich life, making it the highest embodiment of man's culture.

4

I have sketched briefly what I believe to be significant features in the American philosophic tradition. There are, of course, variations among the makers of this tradition, but they are variations on a theme that is characteristically American. The theme is experimental humanism. It is supported by an experimental philosophy that takes inspiration from the knowledge won by the methods of modern science. It is strengthened by a personal morality that is opposed to the ethics of self-love. It is backed by a theory of political morality that posits its faith in the right of men to be free, to be different, but to be equal in governing themselves as best they can.

Other countries with developed intellectual traditions but without popular support, or with strong religious traditions but without technological support, tend to decry those aspects of the American experience that deal with power, action, and technology. As a result, they censure our supposed indifference to ideals. This appraisal fails to recognize the spiritual element in the concept of free men advancing their own way of life unfettered by inflexible inherited systems of religious or class belief. The American philosophic tradition, as I view it, advances a program of strategic ideals which neither strips man of spirit nor promises paradise on earth. It embraces men in the mass without making them mass men. It advances a conception of man and society which is universal in its appeal and which can and should be used to win the minds and hearts of men everywhere.

The perspective I have proposed gears us to an American philosophy which clearly connects our power with moral ends.

I am aware that this perspective may be taken for propaganda. But I cannot believe that it is propaganda to be appreciative of the American tradition of a free society, just as I cannot think it a breach of loyalty to be conscious of the mistakes we have made. I am aware of the fact that when one uses a term like "moral ends," there are always the tough "realists" who understand by it moral pretense. I think it true that we have sometimes invoked a kind of inflated moralism which has been pernicious. The Atlantic Charter, for example, made large promises which worked a temporary magic of words and hopes. But they were not tied to strategic means and slipped quietly into the dark waters whence they arose. We cannot correct these mistakes by rejecting "moral ends." The tough "realists," in their way, offer only another form of pernicious counsel by promoting a philosophy of power unrelated to social consequences or to long-range effects upon the national interest and character. Yalta is an instance of this kind of supposedly realistic American policy. We cannot succeed in effectual world leadership simply by flexing our muscles and pressuring the world with our power—our material and financial power. The American advocates of power politics seem to be more moral-shy than gun-shy. I would urge that we remember that there is immoral power and that even Machiavelli warned "That We Must Avoid Being Despised and Hated."

I believe that there exists a vital American philosophic tradition which may, if we choose, continue to serve us as a strategic guide in meeting the future. But it will play no viable part in our future unless historians and philosophers understand and advance it, unless American philosophers acquire a love for and knowledge of American history, and American historians acquire a love for and knowledge of American philosophy. We have an opportunity to think, to write, and to act in such a way that our joint efforts may throw light on the great issues of our time.

5

The main theme of the essays can now be summed up. The republican experiment was a success and can still serve as a model to all the world, as the founding fathers hoped, because they, by their joint activity, saw the necessity for the constant balance and tension of power and morals. Franklin by his scientific and political activity first illustrated this balance in his underlying orientation of pragmatic wisdom. Jefferson contributed the most searching statement of the equal rights of man in terms that he intended to be a common human faith. Hamilton contributed the most searching statement of the strategic means for establishing the economic basis for a society that could operate as a unity in controlling the resources of nature to increase national productivity. These two in their strong but complementary opposition contributed the strategic ideal of an extensive republic, a federation which has more than purely national significance in the contemporary world. Jefferson alone might have committed us to weaker union by his heightened sense of personal liberty and states' rights, and his idealization of the independent farmer. Hamilton alone might have committed us to an oppressively strong union by his heightened sense of concentrated economic and military power and his idealization of the moneyed class. Their dialectic opposition and argument, together with their strong personal qualities and great talents, resulted in securing the national interest for the common pursuit of happiness. The balance between Hamiltonian power and Jeffersonian morals was given further operational validity by the far-reaching political thought and moderating personal influence of Adams and Madison. These two joined in developing the governmental procedures for balancing power against power in order to promote liberty and protect the rights of the people. Adams developed the constitutional argument for the system of checks and balances among the executive, legislative, and judiciary organs. In particular, he argued against the supremacy of the legislative by providing for the veto power of the executive, the independence of the judiciary, and the division of representation and function within the two legislative branches. Madison developed the constitutional argument for the federal system of an extensive republic to provide for both majority rule and minority rights.

What is the significance of this republican theme for a world threatened by the aggressive total power of the Soviet Union? First, that we ourselves must not respond—mechanically, tropistically, behavioristically—to this total power by adopting the power program of the new Machiavellians. This would not only be seriously in conflict with the living tradition established by the founding fathers but would also neglect one of the greatest sources of power in human history—moral ideals. Power without morals, though it may have a short-run success, fails to secure and combine the strength that resides in free men pursuing a course to protect, defend, and advance their common good. This is not only a compelling moral ideal, it is also a natural characteristic of man as a human being, a realistic and powerful force for undoing the oppression that exists in a total society. For a total society does not yet embrace the world, and there are cities, areas, and climes in which the oppressed can take refuge and from which they can take hope. Western Berlin may be weak, economically, because it is denied access to the natural resources that were a part of its economic organization, but as long as we support it to compensate for this weakness it remains an active symbol of freedom from fear and terror—a symbol that causes hundreds of thousands of refugees to escape from the East and many more who remain within the Iron Curtain to resist the efforts of the Communist tyrants. This, I think, is the meaning of the constant purges, the growing necessity for slave labor, the repeated cries for iron unity as each iron god is dethroned.

Of course, morals without power are weak, just as power without morals spells long-run destruction. The meaning of a program which balances the ever-shifting claims and conditions of power and morals for a policy of international relations should now be apparent. We must not be weak but must strengthen *all* our defenses—military, material, economic, political, social, and moral. And we must strengthen the defenses of that part of the world which is still open to persuasion in the cause of liberty. Both these programs involve real problems, real tensions, and a balancing of means and ends, with the ultimate objective of moving in the direction of more liberty. This means that one must reject a program that keeps us on the brink of preventive war, that one must suspect any total formula for liberation, that one must require more than the ambiguous formula of "the national interest," that one must always recognize the necessity for uneasy compromise with the world and the people as they are, always changing. But as Jefferson said, at the end of his life, the only unchanging objectives are the inherent and unalienable rights of man.

Our confidence in the democratic experiment has weathered a corrosive period of distress when many Americans were deceived by totalitarian talk of our slowness to act. Today, Jefferson's faith will find devout acceptance in a wider immediate circle than even he dreamed of:

Convinced that the republican is the only form of government which is not eternally at open or secret war with the rights of mankind, my prayers and efforts shall be cordially distributed to the support of that we have so happily established. It is indeed an animating thought, that while we are securing the rights of ourselves and our posterity, we are pointing out the way to struggling nations, who wish like us to emerge from their tyrannies also. Heaven help their struggles, and lead them, as it has done us, triumphantly through them.

Lead us with them, we now must add, for our future is not assured.

Index

Act of Toleration, 24
Adams, Abigail, 75, 83, 100
Adams, Henry, 101
Adams, John, 1, 6-7, 10, 12-13, 35,
    43, 65, 66, 71-74, 78, 81-102,
    124, 126-127, 142-143, 149-150
  administration of, 94-96
  cabinet, 72-73, 94-95
  character of, 66, 81
  Hamilton controversy, 71-74
  importance to Revolution, 84-87
  political philosophy, 81-83, 88-
    94, 149-150
  retirement, 96-103
  writings:
    autobiography, 83-84, 96
    Braintree Resolutions, 84
    *Defence of the Constitutions
      of Government of the
      United States of America,
      A,* 88, 90, 92-93
    diary and memoirs, 9
    Discourses on Davila, 92-93
    *Dissertation on the Canon and
      Feudal Law,* 84
    Jefferson correspondence, 97-
      98
    papers, 9, 11
    Thoughts on Government, 86-
      87

Adams, John Quincy, 74, 96, 100-
  101
Adams, Samuel, 84, 85, 99
Age of Experiments, 21
Agriculture, 52, 54, 101, 116, 149
Albany Plan of Union, 20
Alien and Sedition Laws, 64-65,
  112
American:
  capitalism, 51-53, 77-79
  Enlightenment, 3-4, 10, 20, 24,
    43
  experiment, 2-3, 8, 10, 12, 21, 42,
    102, 104, 129-132, 144-145,
    150-151
  foreign policy, 51, 148-151
  history, 3, 80, 103, 138-141, 145-
    149
  industrial economy, 52-58
  philosophy, 3, 21-23, 131, 138-
    141, 145-149
  tradition, 2, 9, 12, 58, 79, 122-
    135, 139, 148-149
American Philosophical Society,
  15, 21
Annapolis Convention, 7
Aristocracy, 62, 89, 91-93, 97, 99
Aristotle, 4, 58, 130-131
Army, 61-62, 68, 73, 75-77, 85, 90,
  95

Articles of Confederation, 6, 110, 117

Bacon, Francis, 4, 14-15, 21, 29, 67, 141
Banks, 53, 56
  national, 55, 111
Beard, Charles, 27
Becker, Carl, 3
Bentham, Jeremy, 17-18
Bill of Rights, 41-42, 109, 114-115, 120
Boorstin, Daniel, 3
Braintree Resolutions, 84
Burr, Aaron, 66, 77, 102
Butterfield, Lyman, 11

"Caesar," 64
Caesar, Julius, 67, 75, 76, 89
Cardanus, 18-19
"Cato," 64
Charron, Pierre, 32-34
Checks and balances, 83, 88-89, 143, 150
Clinton, George, 64
Cohen, I. Bernard, 15
Colonies, 28-29, 83
  colonial experience, 124-125
Communism, 2
  philosophy, 120, 140
  propaganda, 114
  see also Soviet Union
Confederation, 41, 52, 106, 142
Congress:
  Continental, 7, 61, 72, 85-87
  of the United States, 9, 65, 96, 104, 109, 111-112, 120
    House of Representatives, 89, 91
    Senate, 89, 91
Constitutional Convention, 6-7, 21, 41, 58, 62-63, 65, 104, 106, 111, 117, 120
Constitution of the United States, 6-8, 21, 27, 40-41, 52, 55, 58, 63-64, 76, 88, 100, 104, 106-107, 114-116, 132

implied powers or "broad" interpretation, 52, 55, 111
  "strict" interpretation, 111
Continental Congress, 7, 61, 72, 85-87

Declaration of Independence, 25-31, 49, 86, 102, 126
Defence of the Constitutions of Government of the United States of America, A, 88, 90, 92-93
De la Sagesse, 32-34
Democracy, 8, 10, 12, 24, 39-40, 44, 48, 56-59, 66, 88-90, 93, 99, 103, 113-116, 118-119, 126, 131-137, 140, 145, 151
  see also Republican government
Despotism, 40, 46-47
Dewey, John, 23, 131, 146-147
Dickinson, John, 85
Dictatorship, 8, 144
Discourses on Davila, 92-93
Dissertation on the Canon and Feudal Law, A, 84
Doctrinaire liberalism, 24, 42
Du Pont de Nemours, P. S., 54

Editing, contemporary projects, 9-12
Education, 35, 39, 43, 101, 130
Edwards, Jonathan, 14, 29
Electricity, 16
Embargo Acts:
  of 1793, 70
  of 1807, 96-97
Emerson, Ralph Waldo, 145
Empire for liberty, 48, 144-145
Empiricism, 5, 14-17
Engels, Frederick, 143-144
Enlightenment, 3, 10
  American, 3-4, 10, 20, 24, 43
Epicureanism, 19, 31
Equality, 26, 43, 45, 91-92, 122, 126-128, 133-134
Equal rights of man, 8, 23, 28, 119-120, 149

Essay Concerning Human Under-standing, 28-31
Essay on Inequality, 92
Europe, 43, 47, 136
    current importance of Western, 117-118
    see also under individual countries
Excise taxes, 70
Executive power, 65, 89, 91, 114, 149-150
Experimental humanism, 5, 20-21, 146-147
Experimentalism, 131
Experimental naturalism, 15

Factions, 7, 65, 82, 107-109, 113-117, 143, 150
    Madison's theory of, 107-109, 113-117, 143, 150
Farmer, 52, 54, 101, 116, 149
Federalist Papers, 7, 60-62, 72, 106-109, 120
Federalist Party, 7, 50, 65, 69-74, 94-95, 102, 111-112
    Hamiltonian wing, 94-95
    of New England, 97
Federalists, The, 78
Floridas, 73
Foreign policy, 51, 135-137, 148-150
France, 54, 65, 72-73, 83, 87, 92, 95
Franklin, Benjamin, 10, 14-22, 58, 87, 127, 131, 145, 149
    contrast to Edwards, 14
    place in American tradition, 21-22, 149
    political thought, 20-21
    scientific activity, 15-16
    views on morality, 16-19
    writings:
        Autobiography, 21
        papers, 9, 11
        "Parable against Persecution, A," 21
        "Rules by Which a Great Empire May Be Reduced to a Small One," 20
Freedom of press, 39, 41-42, 112

Freedom of religion, 24, 41, 48, 90, 110, 119-120, 124
Freedom of speech, 39, 42, 142
Freedom of thought, 44, 110, 129, 131-135, 142
French Revolution, 88, 92-93

Great Britain, 28, 54, 62, 69-70, 83-84, 87, 95
Greek classics and philosophers, 31-32
    see also under individual philosophers

Habeas corpus, 41
Hacker, Louis, 78-79
Hamilton, Alexander, 1, 6-7, 10, 50-80, 83, 94-96, 101-102, 106-108, 110-112, 149
    character, 65-77
    economic program, 54-55, 110-112
    economic theory, 52-58
    historical reputation, 50-52, 78-80
    political views, 59-66, 77, 149
    relations with Washington and Adams, 68-74
    role in government, 69-73
    writings:
        Army Pay Book, 67-68
        "Caesar" letters, 64
        Federalist Papers, 60-62, 72
        papers, 9, 11
        Public Conduct and Character of John Adams, Esq., President of the United States, The, 73-74
        Report on Manufactures, 54
Harrington, Thomas, 87, 91
Hartz, Louis, 3
Heavenly City of the Eighteenth-Century Philosophers, The, 3
Hedonism, 30
Hegelian dialectic, 122
Helvetius, Claude, 32, 92
Hobbes, Thomas, 32, 76

Holmes, Justice Oliver Wendell, 116
House of Representatives, 89, 91
Humanism, 5, 30, 32-35, 44
Hume, David, 62
Hutchinson, Anne, 124

Industrial economy, 50-59, 149
Instrumentalism, 131, 146
Intellectual freedom, 44, 110, 129, 131-135, 142

Jacobin clubs, 71
James, William, 146
Jay, John, 64, 83
Jefferson, Thomas, 1, 6-7, 10, 13, 21-50, 54, 58-59, 66-67, 69-75, 78, 79, 83, 93-94, 96-100, 102-103, 109, 111-112, 126-127, 129-131, 142-144, 149, 151
    agrarian outlook, 54, 149
    concept of freedom, 38-44
    concept of happiness, 32-38
    importance of, 23, 149
    moral philosophy, 28-31, 44
    personal relations, 34-36
    political philosophy, 24-28, 38-49, 149
    Secretary of State, 69-70
    social philosophy, 36-49
    ties with Locke, 24-31, 67
    view of human nature, 26-38
    writings:
        Adams correspondence, 97-98
        Commonplace Book, 68
        Declaration of Independence, 25-31, 49, 86, 102, 126
        First Inaugural Address, 74
        "Life and Morals of Jesus of Nazareth, The," 32
        Papers of Thomas Jefferson, The, 9-11
Jesus, 5, 18, 32
    "Life and Morals of Jesus of Nazareth, The," 32
    Sermon on the Mount, 98
Judiciary, 83, 149-150
Junto, 16

Laissez faire, 52, 85
Legislative power, 88, 114
Lenin, Nikolai, 2
"Liberty and Power," 110
Locke, John, 14, 24-31, 38, 67, 87
    Essay Concerning Human Understanding, 28-31
    Letter on Toleration, 24
    Second Treatise on Civil Government, 27
Louisiana purchase, 48, 97
    territory, 73

Machiavelli, Niccolo, 76, 148
Madison, James, 1, 6-7, 10, 13, 23, 35, 42-43, 46, 48, 63-64, 66, 73-74, 102-121, 128-129, 142-145, 149-150
    historical contribution, 103-105, 149-150
    political philosophy, 105-106, 113-121, 128-129, 149-150
    under Washington's administration, 109-112
    view in Federalist Papers, 106-109
    view of religion, 119-120
    writings:
        "Consolidation," 109
        Federalist Papers, 106-109, 120
        "Liberty and Power," 110
        National Gazette articles, 109-110
        papers, 9, 11
        "Property," 110
        "Public Opinion," 109
        "Tenth Federalist," 107-108
Magna Carta, 133
Majority rule, 40, 43, 104, 109, 115, 133-134, 142-144, 150
Marshall, John, 51-52, 65
Marx, Karl, 27, 56, 80, 114-115, 143-144
Massachusetts Constitution, 82, 87
Mather, Cotton and Increase, 124
Mercantilism, 52, 85
Metaphysics, 16-18, 33
Mill, John Stuart, 113-114, 142

Minority rights, 104, 109, 115, 149
Mitchell, Broadus, 79-80
Mixed government, 89-91
Monarchy, 47, 62, 77, 81, 93, 99
Moneyed men, 53, 55, 61, 77, 149
Montesquieu, 109
Morgenthau, Hans, 78

Napoleon, 46, 75, 95
National debt, 55-56, 110-111
National Gazette articles, 109-110
National Historical Publications
    Commission, 9
    program of editing, 9-12
Newburgh Affair, 61-62
New conservatism, 51
New England Congregationalism,
    87, 124
New England democracy, 82
New Jersey plan, 63
Newton, Sir Isaac, 14, 29, 67
    Newtonian system, 14

Otis, James, 83-84, 99

Paine, Thomas, 81, 93
Papers of Thomas Jefferson, The,
    9-11
Parliament, 20, 24, 83, 85
    House of Commons and House
        of Lords, 62
Parrington, Vernon, 27
Peace, 45-47, 95, 118-119
Peirce, Charles Sanders, 145-146
People's democracy, 118, 144
Philosopher-king, 113
Physiocrats, 52, 54
Pickering, Timothy, 51, 72
Plato, 4, 89, 115, 145
Political parties, 6-7, 9, 89, 107
    see also Federalist Party *and*
        Republican Party
Pragmatic wisdom, 15-21, 42, 149
Pragmatism, 5, 131, 146
Priestley, Joseph, 18, 98
Property, 27, 54, 56-57, 77, 110
    rights of, 27, 52, 108, 110

*Public Conduct and Character of
    John Adams, Esq., President
    of the United States, The,* 73-
    74
Public credit, 55-56, 110-111
Public opinion, 46, 109
Puritans, 124, 125
    theology of, 14, 99
Pursuit of happiness, 23, 25-49,
    103-105, 126, 130-131, 134, 149

Quakers, 85
    principles of, 47

Report on Manufactures, 54
Republican government, 1, 8, 20,
    28, 60, 66, 82, 86, 88, 90, 99,
    105, 107, 115, 133-135, 151
    see also Democracy
Republican Party, 7, 50, 65, 72, 94,
    96-97, 102-104, 109-112
Revolutionary War, 5, 25, 47, 55,
    68, 71-72
Ricardo, David, 53
Rights of man, 5, 23, 25-28, 37, 44-
    45, 119-121, 126, 131, 142, 150-
    151
Rights of Man, 81, 93
Role of expert, 59
Rousseau, Jean Jacques, 92
Royal Society, 15
Rush, Benjamin, 94

Sabine, George, 140
Say, J. B., 54
Science, 4, 11, 15-16, 21-22, 25, 46,
    146-147
Sedition Law, 64-65, 112
Separation of church and state,
    114, 119-120
Separation of powers, 114-115
Shays's Rebellion, 88
Smith, Adam, 52-54
Socrates, 5, 18, 141
Soviet Union, 2, 50-51, 118-119,
    149
    see also Communism
Stamp Act, 20, 84

State governments, 60
States' rights, 63, 112, 149
Stoicism, 18-19, 31, 36

Technology, 15, 53, 129, 147
Theology, 16-17, 20, 98-99
Ticknor, George, 32-33
Tocqueville, Alexis de, 125
Toleration, 24, 98, 100, 135, 142
Trial by jury, 41, 133
Tyranny, 31, 40-41, 46, 88, 93, 99, 105, 109, 114, 124, 132, 141-143, 150-151

Union of the states, 5, 60, 68, 86, 97, 104, 109, 114, 121, 149
Unitarian(ism), 89, 98
University of Virginia, 35
Utilitarianism, 15, 146

Virginia and Kentucky Resolutions, 112
Virginia plan, 63

War, 46-47, 67-68, 72-73, 95, 150
Washington, George, 5, 8, 55, 61-63, 68-73, 76, 85, 104, 111
  cabinet of, 66, 69-70
  first administration, 6, 68-70
  second administration, 70-71
Weber, Max, 15
Whiskey Rebellion, 70-71
White, Leonard, 78
Williams, Roger, 124
Workshop of liberty, 105, 121, 128-132, 136-137, 145
Wythe, George, 86

XYZ Affair, 95